WHEN BANK SYSTEMS FAIL

Debit Cards, credit cards, ATMs, mobile and online banking: your rights and what to do when things go wrong

Stephen Mason

To the staff at HSBC in Biggleswade

No 2 in the Your Rights series

By the same author
Books
Electronic Signatures in Law
E-mail, networks and the internet:
A concise guide to compliance with the law

eBook
The Millennium Bug: A guide to the legal issues for business

General editor
Electronic Evidence
International Electronic Evidence

Fiction
Under the nom de plume Felix M Temple
The World's a Minefield

Disclaimer
This work is not intended to be comprehensive and is intended to be a general guide to the law and cannot be a substitute for appropriate legal advice. Neither the author not the publisher accept any responsibility for loss occasioned to any person acting or refraining from acting as a result of material contained in this publication. The comments or views expressed by the author are not necessarily the comments or views of any organisation in which the author is employed.

© Stephen Mason 2014   All rights reserved.
Stephen Mason has asserted his right under the Copyright, Designs and Patents Act 1988 to be identified as Author of this work.

Book ISBN 9781858117218
EBook 9781858117225   Printed & typeset in the UK

PP Publishing
Suite 74, 17 Holywell Hill
St Albans AL1 1DT, UK   www.peerpractice.co.uk

Contents

Ackowledgements v

Chapter 1	Introduction	3
Chapter 2	How the ATM system works	5
Chapter 3	How thieves steal from ATMs and other devices	15
Chapter 4	The weaknesses of internet banking systems	29
Chapter 5	The contract with the bank	39
Chapter 6	Negligence of the bank and the customer	47
Chapter 7	The legal basis for a claim	67
Chapter 8	Some problems with evidence	73
Chapter 9	Handling a dispute in the early stages	79
Chapter 10	What to do when disputes occur	83

Appendices

1	Actions you should consider taking immediately where you have a problem with an ATM and PIN or a Point of Sale (PoS) purchase	98
2	Excerpts from the Home Office Counting Rules for fraud and forgery	104
3	Suggested text of a letter to send to the bank before taking legal action	105
4	Sample Particulars of Claim for an Internet banking claim	108
5	Sample of a Particulars of Claim for an ATM or Point of Sale (PoS) claim	112
6	Some questions to ask a solicitor before instructing them	116
7	Some questions to ask of the card issuer if the card issuer has not provided the information at the disclosure stage of legal proceedings	119
8	Guidance issued to customers on reducing ATM and on-line banking crime	127
9	Fraud Figures	130
10	'Debit cards, ATMs and negligence of the bank and customer'	134
11	'Electronic banking and how courts approach the evidence'	163
12	Further Information	181

Index 195

Acknowledgments

The chapters covering the technical issues relating to ATMs and online banking have not altered since the first edition, and they were written with the extensive help of the following, each of which improved the text and educated me further: Ross Anderson, Professor of security engineering at the University of Cambridge; Mike Bond; Graeme Burnett (a member of the Association for Computing Machinery); Omar Choudary; Ken Lindup; Jim McClymont; Steven J. Murdoch and Matthew Pemble. I owe each a debt of gratitude for their invaluable assistance. I also thank Nicholas Bohm. who has the kindness to offer valuable comments when requested.

Notwithstanding my thanks to those mentioned above. the author remains solely responsible for the text.

The case studies taken from *Ombudsman News* are included with the permission of the Office of the Financial Ombudsman Service.

The author granted the consumer organisation *Which?* a licence to place an earlier version of the letter in appendix 3 as a free download from the *Which?* website in November 2011.

Please note, the content of this book only covers the law in England and Wales.

Chapter 1
Introduction

The use of information technology by the banks has changed the service they offered so much, that it is difficult to recall what banking was like, even twenty years ago.

However, new risks came with the benefits of information technology. It took a while for criminals to work out how to exploit the weaknesses. But once the use of the internet became widespread, criminals were able to take advantage of this new source of information, including knowledge about how to take advantage of weaknesses in the security of electronic banking systems and equipment. There are now markets that sell specialised know-how and equipment to criminal enterprises, and information is traded to facilitate the misappropriation of identity and other attacks on financial systems.

Only the banks (and the successful criminals) really know how electronic banking systems work and what the weak points are, and the banks prefer to keep their weaknesses secret. Some banks are even reluctant to accept that employees can be the cause of theft. There are cases where an employee changes the address of the customer, then orders a new card to be sent to the new address. The employee or their accomplices then use the card to steal money from the customer's account. This happened to Emma Woolf. This means that when a customer suffers a loss, the bank might deny that its systems could have been at fault. As a result, the bank may blame the customer for the loss, and refuse to refund the money. Because the technical issues are complex, that leaves the customer at a significant disadvantage. This book is intended to help reduce this disadvantage.

The vast majority of transactions carried out through the banking systems work without fault. However, when money is debited from an account without the knowledge or authority of the customer, the response by the bank can often be a stressful and chastising experience for the customer.

There are four important observations to make about banking methods that use information technology:

First, the banks have consistently, ever since the first IT systems were developed, insisted that their systems are never at fault. It usually takes a researcher or team of researchers, usually at a university, to expose weaknesses in banking systems.

Second, even if those members of security staff in a bank are aware of the vulnerabilities, they tend not to reveal their knowledge of them, which means customers are often unfairly held responsible for transactions of which they have no knowledge.

Third, regulators and organisations such as the Financial Ombudsman Service often accept uncritically the assertions by the banks about the assurance of the security and integrity of their IT systems, largely to the detriment of customers with legitimate concerns.

Finally, legal systems (in many countries) have failed customers when they have taken legal action to recover funds that have been stolen by thieves:

> 1. All too often, banks have succeeded in telling customers to destroy evidence (that is, to destroy their bank card) with impunity and with no sanction from the courts.
>
> 2. The banks often oppose the disclosure (or discovery) of important evidence held by the bank from being brought to court that they claim is either not necessary or confidential.
>
> 3. Sometimes decisions are made that in effect label an honest customer as liar when making a claim, particularly when the customer is adamant that they did not write down their PIN (personal identity number) and the PIN was not with the card that was stolen and subsequently successfully used by the thief. The aim of a bank in litigation is to hide the weaknesses of the banking systems, which is partly why decisions are made that are based on a false understanding of the strengths and weaknesses of the technology.

This is demonstrated in the Norwegian case of Paal Øiestad:

> Paal Øiestad and his family were in Rome in September 2008 on holiday, when a credit card was stolen and over Nok 50,000 taken before it was cancelled. Mr Øiestad insisted that the code was not written down, because it had been committed to memory. The bank argued before the Norwegian Complaints

Board and the District Court that the customer had acted with gross negligence by allegedly keeping the PIN together with the stolen card. The bank won the case before both the Complaints Board and District Court. Mr Øiestad appealed – he insisted that he was not a liar. While waiting for the appeal hearing, Mr Øiestad received a letter from the bank, dated 12 June 2012, admitting it was wrong, apologising, and agreeing to pay his legal costs. This case, together with a translation of the letter, is the subject of an article by Maryke Silalahi Nuth and published in the 2012 issue of the *Digital Evidence and Electronic Signature Law Journal*.

The purpose of this book
This book is aimed at the customer that has suffered a loss from their account, either an online banking account or by way of an ATM or a point of sale terminal (as found in shops, restaurants and garages). It provides an introduction to the law and how the technology works at a high level of generality. It is not a substitute for legal books on banking or books on banking technology.

Chapter 2
How the ATM system works

This chapter provides a brief outline of the component parts of the ATM (Automated Teller Machine) system. If you have had money stolen from your account, and the bank says the money was withdrawn from an ATM with the correct PIN (personal identity number) (a PIN is one form of electronic signature), you will need to know how the ATM system works if you decide to challenge the bank. The description set out in this chapter is not comprehensive, partly because each bank will have implemented the ATM systems into their computer systems differently, and partly because the description provided in this part will be subject to changes, because the banks constantly alter their systems to improve security. If you wish to have a more detailed explanation, you will have to conduct further research of your own. You will find a list of further reading to help you in appendix 1.

The basics
The bank issues you with a card and a PIN for use at ATMs and at point-of-sale terminals in shops, garages and restaurants. The card is designed in such a way that it is very difficult for a thief to duplicate a card. It is intended that only you know your PIN. This ought to mean that if somebody obtains your card, even for a short time, they should not be able to have enough information to make a copy, and they should not be able to use it to make cash withdrawals or purchases. The electronic chip on the card is responsible for this.

The card
The components of a card
The card that inserted into ATMs and card readers is made up of three components:

1. The plastic card

2. The chip, which is an embedded microprocessor

3. The magnetic strip

Information stored on the card
The following information is included on the card:

> The principal account number (PAN), and the dates the card is valid (start and expiry dates) are embossed on the face of the card.
>
> The name of the customer.
>
> On the reverse of the card, there is a signature panel containing the signature of the customer, which is used to authenticate the customer.
>
> Also printed on the magnetic strip on the reverse of the card is the Card Verification Value. This number comprises the last four digits of the card number and a three digit 'security' number (CVV2) for use in transactions when the card is not present, such as when you authorise payment over the telephone or the internet. On some cards this is a four figure number on the front of the card.

The chip

The chip is basically a small computer that runs a program for interacting with terminals. The chip on the card will enable the customer to interact with ATMs by withdrawing cash, make payments and conduct transactions on the account. Other types of card include loyalty cards, gift cards and staff discount cards, and the holder of the card can make withdrawals or payments, or add loyalty points, depending on the nature of the card.

The chip contains the following:

> A memory containing the same information that is recorded on the magnetic strip.
>
> The primary account number (PAN) of the customer, which is the long number on the front of the card, usually 16 digits in length, and acts as a unique identifier for each customer.
>
> The sequence number, which allows your bank to distinguish between different cards with the same PAN, so the number is increased by one for each additional card issued. If you have a joint account, the cards may have the same PAN on the front, but they will usually have different sequence numbers; the sequence number is often printed on the front for debit cards.
>
> A copy of your chosen PIN (your bank holds a separate copy). A copy of the PIN is held in the card, and the bank holds the

main record in its database in encrypted form. When you change your PIN, the bank sends a message to the ATM at which you are changing your PIN to tell it to load the new PIN into the card at that moment. In this way, the bank and the card PIN should always stay the same. This is why you cannot change your PIN except at an ATM.

A card authentication key, known as the Unique Derived Key (UDK). This is specific to your card. It is kept secretly and securely within the card, and used by the chip program to prove that it is not a counterfeit.

A combination of symmetric and (sometimes) asymmetric cryptographic keys, and asymmetric certificates. The purpose of these is to enable the ATM to recognise the card, and to enable data to be communicated between the card and the issuing bank securely.

An Application Transaction Counter (ATC). This is a counter that increases by one each time a transaction occurs. This can be an important item of evidence, because if the number on the counter does not match the transaction history recorded by your bank, it might prove that your card was not used in the disputed transactions. For this reason, you should never destroy your card, and the bank should never instruct you to destroy your card.

Additional instructions included by the bank to control the behaviour of the software on the card when it is used offline. For instance, the bank can determine when the card should request an online referral back to the bank.

At the option of the bank, a copy of the data recorded on the magnetic strip.

The magnetic strip

The magnetic strip stores the following data (this is a simplified explanation, because there are three tracks in each magnetic strip):

The card and identification data of the person to whom the card was issued (e.g. card number, name of customer, expiry date, but not an asymmetric cryptographic certificate).

The service code that identifies whether a chip is present on the card and the types of transactions that the card can be used for.

The PIN. By including the PIN on one of the tracks on the magnetic strip, it permits you to use the card in an ATM or card reader which does not have the ability to read the chip, or where the technology in the ATM or card reader is not working properly.

A Card Verification Value (CVV) is added to the magnetic strip. The CVV is computed from the account number and expiry date, then encrypted. This number should never be printed on the card. In theory, by including a CVV, a thief cannot produce a forged card that can convince the bank that it is not forged. However, the CVV is not perfect. The CVV is supposed to be used by the issuing bank to validate the data on the strip. However, the issuing bank does not always check the CVV when the card is inserted into an ATM. The CVV is only additional data, so it does not prevent the data stored on the magnetic strip (including the CVV) from being obtained by a thief using a false ATM.

'Contactless' cards

The banks have added new technology to debit and credit cards. They are called 'contactless cards'. The added technology is called 'near field communication'. Contactless cards have a radio antenna embedded into the plastic. The software on the chip on the card communicates with the software in the terminal in the shop by radio signals. This means that a contactless card can be read through several layers of material, for instance the leather of a handbag or wallet, and a coat. You do not have to use your electronic signature (PIN). The money is deducted from your bank account or added to your credit card bill by waving your card near the terminal.

In effect, having a contactless card is like having cash in your possession, but there will be times when the cash is removed without your knowledge.

The risk

Contactless cards are not without risk. If your card is stolen, it means the thief does not need to know your PIN. They just have to wave the card at terminals in shops, garages and railway stations. There have been instances where customers have presented their ordinary card to the terminal to pay with their PIN, and the money has been deducted from a separate contactless card, which was in their bag or wallet – so the money has been deducted twice.

In June 2012, NatWest bank launched a mobile telephone app called 'Get Cash'. This let customers withdraw money without using a debit card at their ATMs. To obtain the app, customers had to register for online banking, then mobile banking, and download the app to their telephone.

It was reported that one Tim from London had £950 taken from his account in August using a security code downloaded using the app. The money was taken from 11 ATMs in three days, each one below the £100 limit NatWest imposed for each ATM withdrawal without a card. This was not his usual pattern of spending. Tim had never heard of the Get Cash system. He was registered for online banking, but not mobile banking. NatWest then accused him of giving his personal details to a thief, but refunded the £950 as a gesture of goodwill after BBC Radio 4 Money Box contacted NatWest.

Refusing a contactless card

When your card is renewed, you will probably discover that your bank issues you with a replacement card with the contactless chip already on the card. Unless you want to use one of these cards, it is important to ask the bank to issue you with an ordinary card, not a contactless card. You will find that it is difficult to make the bank issue you with an ordinary card. If you ask for an ordinary card, the bank will assert that they do not issue ordinary cards any more. You must be persistent. The bank will issue you with an ordinary card, but not before trying to persuade you that ordinary cards are no longer available.

An overview of the ATM process

The network

In the United Kingdom, VocaLink links most of the ATMs to the banks. VocaLink also provides some issuers of credit and debit cards with the ability to obtain access to overseas ATMs through its connections to the international VISA and MasterCard networks. The brands of cards that can be used in the VocaLink network include PLUS (VISA) and Cirrus (MasterCard).

The ATM

It is possible for an ATM to be owned and managed in a variety of ways, such as:

Owned and managed by the issuing bank.

Owned by the bank and managed by a third party, such as VocaLink.

Owned and managed by a third party, such as a corner shop.

The transaction flow

What follows is a technical description of authenticating the card and authorising payment (also called the transaction flow).

Authentication of the card by the ATM

When your card is inserted into an ATM, the software in the ATM must determine whether the card is capable of interacting with the machine. It is for this reason that the software in the ATM communicates with the software on the card, or the magnetic strip. The ATM and card must be able to communicate with each other, and if they can, you will be presented with the options that you are permitted to carry out on the ATM.

The actions you can carry out with the ATM will depend on whether the ATM is connected to the bank. This is called 'online'. Most ATMs are now 'online'.

Step 1

The software in the ATM communicates with the software on the card to determine which technology it should use for the transaction: whether the magnetic strip or the chip. To establish whether a chip is present, the service code on the magnetic strip on the card is read.

If the card has a chip, the software in the ATM will read the software in the chip.

The ATM will then permit the customer to conduct those transactions that are permitted.

A technical issue of great importance:
When chips for cards were designed, the banks naturally attempted to reduce the possibility that the chip on the card can be forged. The method used by the banks to prevent forgery is called Static Data Authentication, in which a single key is shared between every card issued and the bank. The ATM does

not know the key, and can only communicate with the issuing bank that holds the key if the ATM is online. If the ATM is not connected to the issuing bank, the software in the ATM cannot determine whether the card inserted into the machine is genuine. This means the thief does not need to know the correct PIN, because it is for the chip on the card to verify whether the correct PIN is used, and the thief can program the chip to communicate 'yes' when asked by the ATM if the correct PIN has been used.

Step 2

If the software on the ATM communicates with the software on the chip on the card (presuming the card has a chip, and it is working), the card sends the following data to the ATM:

(i) An Authorisation Request Cryptogram (ARQC), which is generated from the cryptographic keys on the card.

(ii) Data about the transaction, such as the amount and the currency.

(iii) The value of the application transaction counter (ATC).

(iv) An Authorisation Response Cryptogram (ARPC), which is generated by the issuing bank in response to the ARQC. This is a cryptographic response that includes the decision by the bank whether to authorise the request. It is sent back to the card for validation before the transaction is completed.

This is important:
The card is not always verified in all ATM transactions.

What happens when the ATM is online

If the correct PIN is entered, the software stored on the chip (or the magnetic strip) and the software in the ATM terminal communicate with each other to decide whether the transaction needs to be authorised online (if the ATM is not online this will not occur).

Step 3

This method can be used for transactions with both the magnetic stripe and the chip.

The bank decides whether the transaction is valid and sends a response to the terminal and the card.

The transaction

The authorisation system of the issuing bank decides, on the basis of risk analysis, bank policy, and the result of the authentication of the card and verification of the card holder, whether to authorise the transaction. Software in the issuing bank responds to the message stating whether the transaction is authorised. If it is authorised, the ATM will carry out the transaction: that is it will dispense cash. Where a transaction is from the chip, an ARPC will be returned to the card for validation before the transaction is complete.

If the bank approves the transaction, the microprocessor on the card produces a transaction certificate (TC).

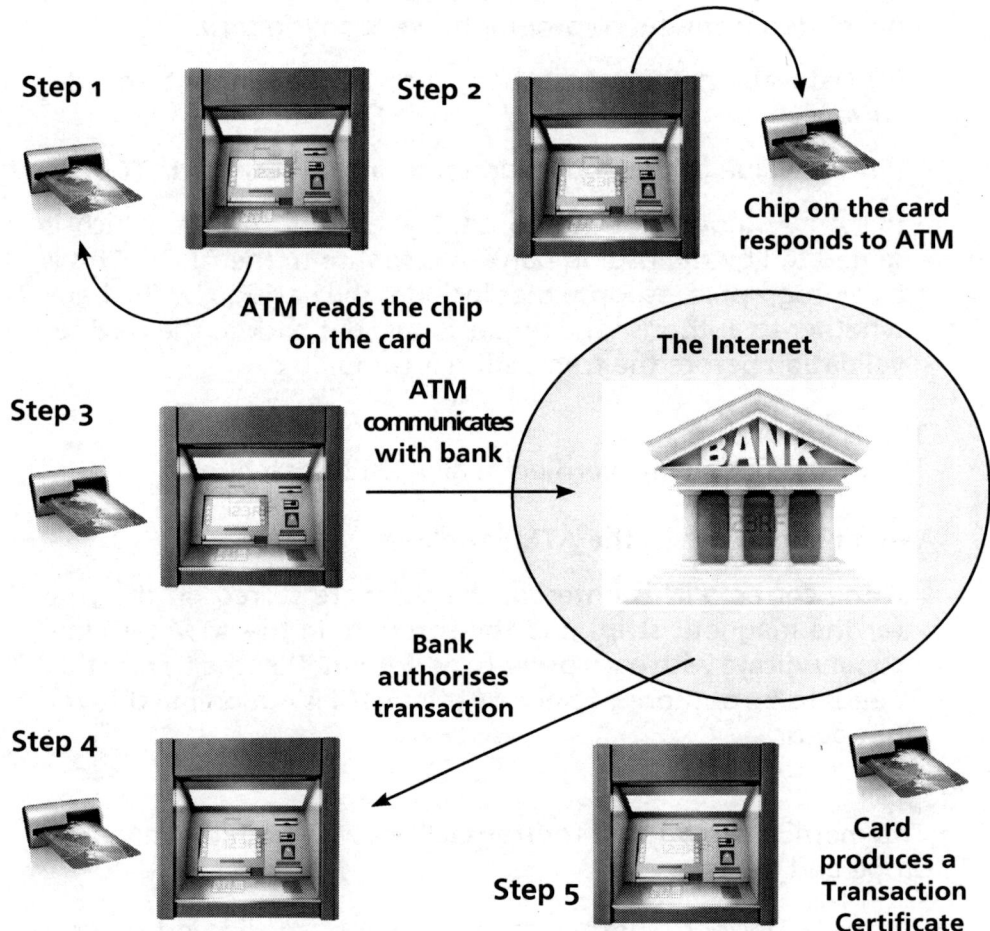

Magnetic strip fallback

There are occasions where the ATM will continue with a transaction without a chip on the card, or without reading the data on the chip:

1. If the devices that reads the chip in the ATM is not working.

2. If there is no chip on the card, or if the software in the ATM cannot read the information on the chip (the chip might be damaged), the ATM may proceed with the transaction based on data read from the magnetic strip.

3. If the microprocessor on the card fails during a transaction, it is possible that 'fallback' will occur, where the software in the ATM will communicate with the software on the magnetic strip, and the ATM will carry out the transaction without any further authentication.

The data sent between the microprocessor and the ATM includes all the information required to make a cloned strip card. This means if a skimming device is installed at an ATM, a forged magnetic strip can be created and used with the correct PIN in an ATM, providing the PIN is also obtained.

When magnetic strip 'fallback' occurs, the ATM will send a message to the issuing bank, indicating that this is a 'fallback' transaction. The magnetic strip data may be sent to the acquiring bank in the clear, although the PIN is always encrypted. One problem for the customer is that often the bank will insist that the chip was read, but sometimes the chip was not read, because the magnetic strip was read instead. This means the card that was used could have been a forged card.

The receipt

Information has begun to appear on debit card and credit card receipts. Below are some of the abbreviations and the possible meaning of each abbreviation – with thanks to Dr Steven J. Murdoch for providing the possible meanings (the author also asked the Payment Council, but there was no reply):

PTID: not known

MID: Merchant Identity

TID: Terminal Identity

EFTSN: (possibly) Electronic Funds Transfer

Authcode: Authorisation code, which comes back after an online authorisation. In the case of a telephone referral, it is typed in at the terminal.

AID: Application Identity, which identifies whether it was Visa/Mastercard/Link

App Eff: The effective date of the application, that is the start date of the card

App Seq: Application sequence number, that is if there are a number of cards with the same account number this distinguishes them

Most of these are almost entirely irrelevant for disputed transactions. More useful information would be the application cryptogram, transaction counter, unpredictable number, terminal verification results, issuer application data, and such like, but these items are rarely on receipts. Of course, you only have this information if you actually used your card and have the receipt; otherwise, if somebody else uses your data and card (if it is stolen or lost), then you will not know this information. However, these details also appear on the merchant receipt, so it is wise to contact the merchant if you have a problem, because they might be willing to help you by providing a copy of their receipt.

The data sent between the microprocessor and the ATM includes all the information required to make a cloned strip card. This means if a skimming device is installed at an ATM, a forged magnetic strip can be created and used with the correct PIN in an ATM, providing the PIN is also obtained.

When magnetic strip 'fallback' occurs, the ATM will send a message to the issuing bank, indicating that this is a 'fallback' transaction. The magnetic strip data may be sent to the acquiring bank in the clear, although the PIN is always encrypted. One problem for the customer, is that often the bank will insist that the chip was read, but sometimes the chip was not read, because the magnetic strip was read instead. This means the card that was used could have been a forged card.

Chapter 3
How thieves steal from ATMs and other devices

In the age of the machine, thieves steal from banks using a variety of techniques and methods. To understand the weaknesses in the machines and the software used by the banks, it is useful to understand how thieves go about their activities. The methods used by criminals can be separated into two stages:

Stage 1

If possible, they obtain the card (and as much information as they can, such as the PIN and security code). If not, they try to obtain enough information associated with the card to enable them to masquerade as the customer.

Stage 2

They then use the information (and the card if they have stolen the card) to:

   1. Make cash withdrawals through ATMs.

   2. Copy the data recorded on the magnetic strip and place this on a blank card to buy items physically through shops and garages, or remotely by way of the internet or over the telephone.

Timing is important, and might affect how the bank deals with complaints that a transaction has occurred for which you are not responsible:

   1. The gap between stage 1 and stage 2 could be very short: if a thief steals your card, he can use it very quickly to make cash withdrawals or buy expensive goods minutes or hours later.

   2. Alternatively, the thief might obtain the information stored on the card by skimming the data from a shop, who might sell the information on to a gang of criminals several weeks or months later, before the second gang (or third or fourth gang) uses the information to buy goods and withdraw cash.

There can be a difference in time between the moment a thief obtains the information from a card and the time they use it. This was illustrated in a programme entitled 'Fraud Squad', which was broadcast on ITV1 on 5 April 2012 between 9 and 10 pm. The City of London Police and the Dedicated Cheque and Plastic Crime Unit were followed during the course of three cases of criminal gangs from Romania, filmed stealing from

ATMs. One of the gangs operated a business buying stolen information and cloning imported blank cards with the stolen information, so they could then steal from bank accounts weeks or months after the information was obtained from the legitimate card.

If you have had your card stolen, the thieves usually combine stages 1 and 2, by stealing as much money or by buying as many goods as they can immediately, before you have the opportunity to inform the bank. A frequent method used by thieves is to tamper with ATMs with the purpose of retaining your card or cash, so you then leave the ATM, and they wait until you are gone before they return to retrieve your card or cash moments later.

However, if your card has always remained in your possession, and you have not had cash retained in an ATM, but you continue to experience withdrawals of cash that you have not authorised or made, it is probable that one set of thieves have obtained the information stored on your card in stage 1, then dealt with your information separately in a similar way outlined above, in stage 2.

There are also physical attacks on ATMs, and a mix of other methods including the production of physical items (such as a false front) to make it appear a customer is interacting with the legitimate ATM, and taking advantage of the weaknesses in the software to by-pass security. Some of these methods only occur once, and some occur all the time. Where a method is used frequently, it is arguable that the banks should be made to redesign the hardware to deal with well-known methods of undermining the machines.

There is also a difference between the risks that the banks can control and the risks that you must understand and control. For instance, the use of social engineering is used to obtain information from you. However, the bank cannot control how you respond to an attempt by a thief to obtain information about your bank card. The banks can (and do with varying degrees of efficiency) alert customers to the various methods used by criminals, but the bank cannot act for you in such circumstances.

It is important to realise that the discussion below lists a number of methods that thieves have used, and some theoretical methods that could be used. Although the police and banks might not have seen evidence of some of the methods described below, it does not mean that the criminals have not been successful in using the methods that might appear to be only possible in theory at present. It must also be understood that the banks are constantly trying to improve security, and the thieves also develop new methods to undermine any new form of security put in place by the banks. This means that the methods used to steal cards and the information recorded on cards does not remain static.

The risks under the control of the bank
Immediate methods of stealing

Thieves steal from ATMs using a variety of methods. These methods do not apply to customers, but are included for the sake of completeness. For instance, an ATM might be smashed or physically lifted from its location by the use of heavy machinery such as an excavator. Examples of such attacks include:

> An ATM might be physically removed by force from its location, also called a 'ram raid'. This method tends to be used to steal ATMs from shops.

> An ATM might be broken open in situ using gas, explosives or cutting equipment.

> People replenishing the ATM might be physically attacked.

> Customers using the ATM might be forced to give up their card and PIN for fear of their life. People have been killed for their PIN. In February 2007, two men living in Manchester murdered a 62-year-old security guard after he refused to reveal his PIN, and in July 2008, police believe that two French students, Laurent Bonomo and Gabriel Ferez, were tortured to death for the PIN on their cards.

Employees that steal

Although this chapter only deals with the ATM system, it is important to be aware of another very important weakness: employees that steal. Employees of the bank can be responsible for stealing from customers. An employee can change your address, then authorise a new card to be sent to the new address. The employee or their accomplices can then use the card to steal from your account. Some banks do not keep proper records of changes of address, so often a bank will refuse to accept that this might have occurred, although most banks now have audit trails on their computer systems that are designed to record each change of address. This happened to Emma Woolf.

Emma Woolf discovered that someone was taking money from her business account with the Abbey by making cash withdrawals from an ATM near their home in London. In all, £10,000 was stolen. Abbey was subsequently taken over by Santander. The bank did not accept responsibility. Jonathan Groman, her fiancée, was suspected of withdrawing the money.

Employees of the bank asserted that the card was not cloned, and the correct PIN was used, and it was further asserted that Emma Woolf or Jonathan Groman were responsible for the transactions. Emma Woolf had no other recourse other than to take legal action to recover the money.

Some time later, Thames Valley Police entered the home of a suspect in another, unrelated matter. During their search, they found many papers relating to Emma Woolf's Abbey bank account, including the missing statements and cards. The person arrested previously worked at the head office of the Abbey bank. Apparently another customer had £150,000 stolen by the same person.

Santander agreed to refund the stolen money, including her legal fees. The bank refused to admit liability, made it a condition that she had to sign a confidentiality agreement, and would neither apologise to Emma Woolf nor paid Mr Groman any compensation. It appeared that the fraud was committed by changing the address on Emma Woolf's account, sending a new card to the new address, obtaining the PIN from Abbey's records, and then subsequently withdrawing money from ATMs.

One of the authors spoke to Inspector Jacqui Bartlett of the Thames Valley Police Economic Crime Unit by telephone on 19 January 2012 at 10 am to enquire what action the police undertook after the arrest. Apparently no action was taken, and the person was released without charge.

Getting the card and PIN to the customer

The banks decide how the card and PIN are sent to you. One method, which is used in some countries, is where the bank sends the card and PIN to the local branch of your bank. You must then physically collect the card and PIN from your branch. This method does not prevent somebody from impersonating you, but if the bank hands over the card and PIN to a person masquerading as you, the bank is at fault.

In the UK, the postal service is widely used to distribute cards and PINs. There are several ways a criminal can intercept a card and PIN in this context.

1. A corrupt postman or postwoman might recognise the envelope containing the card, and steal the envelope when it is in the hands of the postal service. The same is true of a letter containing the PIN.

2. The envelope containing the card is delivered to the addressee, but the envelope is either intercepted by a thief (for instance, in a block of flats where the post cannot be delivered to an individual flat), or somebody else takes in the envelope, and does not hand it over to the person to whom the envelope is addressed.

3. The card is delivered to the correct address, but you have moved, and failed to inform your bank that you have moved. Either the new occupier might then use the card to steal, or if the envelope is put back into the postal system as 'return to sender', a corrupt postal worker might intercept it.

Duplicate cards

It has been known for a bank or credit card company to issue two identical cards to a customer. Given that this has occurred, it means that the system for producing cards can fail.

Technical problems

The dominant smart card payment system is called the EMV protocol. It is named after EuroPay, MasterCard and Visa, who set it up, and it now maintained by EMVCo, which in turn is owned by American Express, Discover, JCB, MasterCard, UnionPay and Visa. There are flaws in the design of the EMV protocol, some of which are the result of choices made when designing the protocol, some of which are errors of design or how the protocol is implemented. The list below sets out how things can go wrong.

Flaws in verifying the PIN

A thief obtains your card, but they do not know the PIN. A flaw in the design of the EMV protocol allows the thief to use the card without knowing the PIN. The thief performs what is called a 'man-in-the-middle attack' to mislead the software controlling the terminal into believing the PIN is verified correctly, while telling the card that no PIN was entered. This is called the 'no PIN attack'. When you insert your card into the point of sale terminal, you key in the PIN. The software in the terminal then passes the PIN back to the card. The software on the card tells the software in the terminal that the PIN is correct. This communication is not encrypted.

Dr Saar Drimer and Dr Steven J. Murdoch at the University of Cambridge demonstrated in 2009 and in 2011 that a thief can use a small hand-held device, called Smart Card Detective, which intercepts the communication between the card and the terminal. This device allows the thief to key in any PIN, and the software in the terminal will accept it was the correct PIN. It seems that most banks have not yet stopped this very dangerous weakness. What should happen is that the software in the terminal should, ideally, carry out an online check to prevent this attack from occurring.

The 'pre-play' attack
There is another technical flaw that might account for so many people suffering from withdrawals from their account that they claim they are not responsible for. This is called the 'pre-play' attack. To fully understand how it works (as with the other forms of attack mentioned in this book), you will have to download the relevant technical paper, as listed in the relevant appendix. This method relies on flaws in the design and implementation of the EMV protocol. When inserted into an ATM, the software on the card communicates with the software in the ATM. To prevent a transaction from being repeated, an unpredictable number is used to ensure each transaction is unique. In a classic protocol design, the bank should generate the unpredictable number, and the card should authenticate it, together with the amount, the date and the identity number of the ATM. However, it appears that the designers cut corners by requiring the terminal to generate the unpredictable number.

This means that four things are wrong:

1. The terminal can generate a poor unpredictable number, which means that the unpredictable number can be predicted before it is needed, so a thief can obtain data from a card one day and use the data at the ATM the next day.

2. The terminal might only use a counter, so a thief knows that the next number will be.

3. The identity number of the ATM is not authenticated, which makes the attack easier to perform.

4. A thief can manipulate the communications between the terminal and the bank.

These vulnerabilities result in a 'pre-play' attack. This allows an EMV chip card to be skimmed and the information obtained from it can be

used to make withdrawals at a later place and time. It best explains phantom withdrawals where a small number of transactions are made using a card a few hours or days after the customer used their card at a location where their data could have been harvested. It must be emphasised that pre-play attacks do not really explain:

1. scenarios where the card is stolen, that is where card is used without a PIN at an ATM (and neither does the 'no PIN attack');

2. a long series of dozens or hundreds of withdrawals against an account stretching back months.

Software recording 'facts' incorrectly
Sometimes the software in a bank will indicate that a PIN authorised the transaction, but in fact it was actually authenticated by a manuscript signature. The software can report incorrect facts because it is manipulated deliberately, or because there is an error in the software in the terminal.

For instance, a shop assistant might have problems with asking you for a PIN, so they might override the software to ask for a manuscript signature, rather than a PIN. The software in the terminal then informs the bank that a PIN was used. Investigators usually rely on this 'fact' that a PIN was used, even though a manuscript signature was used.

This happened to Rachel Addison in 2012. Five transactions had cleared from her account, and there was a further 25 transactions that were pending. A total of £1,152.30 was taken. Each payment was for £40 or less. Barclays insisted that a new debit card had been sent to her, but she did not receive it. Barclays also insisted that the correct PIN had been used. This meant that she was liable for the full amount. Eventually, the fraud team at Barclays discovered that the transactions were actually authorised by a manuscript signature that was clearly not hers, and not by a PIN.

This is an important point, because in England and Wales, there is a common law presumption that includes computers by implication (or more accurately, digital data). The Law Commission formulated the presumption as follows: 'In the absence of evidence to the contrary, the courts will presume that mechanical instruments were in order at the material time'. The problem with this presumption is that software written by human beings has always been – and continues to be – subject to errors (as described in detail in chapter 5, *Electronic Evidence*). This means it is essential to ensure a judge understands this if you decide to recover money through legal action, because many judges and lawyers assume that you can trust digital evidence because of this presumption.

Reversing the transaction
The thief manipulates the ATM during the transaction to make the software at the bank conclude that the customer did not receive the cash, and therefore re-credits or reverses the transaction. Variants on this include collusion by employees of the bank or ATM network, by which the thief obtains the cash without a record being made.

Another method depends on the fact that there are two transactions that take place when you pay for something using a point of sale terminal. First, you pay via the terminal to authorise the payment of the money to the shop or restaurant (called a merchant). Then a separate transaction occurs between the merchant and the bank, where the bank pays the merchant. Thieves noticed that when you keyed in your PIN, the software authenticate the transaction with the bank. However, the identity of the merchant is not authenticated. A thief would buy goods from a shop, then reverse the transaction, which put the money back into their account.

Theft of deposits
Various techniques are used to enable the perpetrator to obtain cash where you are led to believe that you have deposited money in a machine that is successfully validated, but in fact no such transaction has taken place.

Undermining encryption methodologies – obtaining the correct PIN
After you type in the PIN, the number is communicated to the bank for checking. Each PIN is usually formatted into a 64-bit block, and encrypted under a secret shared key. Each bank will have a different method of formatting the PIN into the 64-bit block, and will use different encryption keys. This is important, because the PIN is routed through different zones in the ATM network, and the PIN

will need to be re-formatted and re-encrypted several times before it reaches the bank's computer.

The problem is that some encryption methodologies are flawed. This is because by manipulating the contents of the 64-bit block in which the PIN is hidden, it is possible to obtain a PIN in approximately 24 guesses, and once the thief has tried a number of times and been successful, they can reduce the number of guesses to 15. This method can only be used if a person has access to the hardware security module, which is a physical device that is included in the ATM.

Relay interception
If a thief can tamper with a card reader, then it is possible to use the data from a card for fraudulent purposes. The method is this: The customer goes into a shop or restaurant in which the card reader has been tampered with. When the card is inserted or swiped and the customer types in their PIN, the software in the terminal forwards all the details (card details and PIN) to a thief over the internet. The thief then uses the card details to buy expensive items (e.g. a diamond or a motor cycle), or even to withdraw cash from an ATM, although this would be technically more difficult. The shop or restaurant, if it is controlled by thieves, might give the customer dinner or lunch for free, which means the customer has no tangible evidence that they actually visited the shop or restaurant.

The problem with the effectiveness of this method is that a thief will begin to use the data to enact transactions immediately, usually over the internet. This makes it difficult for the customer to demonstrate that they were not responsible for the transactions made by the thief, unless the transactions were very closely associated in time or geographically very far apart.

The risks partly under the control of the bank that you should be aware of
Trapping and stealing cash at the ATM

Thieves can place a false front on the ATM. This enables you to carry out a transaction, but the false front prevents the cash from being dispensed, or it makes it appear that you have removed the cash.

Trapping and stealing the card

The thief places a device over an ATM to physically retain your card after you key in the PIN as you use the ATM. You can give instructions to the ATM, but the device prevents the ATM from returning the card. The thief recovers the card when you leave the ATM, and it is used to conduct fraudulent transactions (although the thief will need the PIN). This is also called the 'Lebanese Loop'. Variations of this theme include where the thief distracts the customer and successfully obtains the card by exchanging it with a card that looks like your card, called the 'Algerian V trap'. Another example is where thieves insert a sticky board covered with powerful glue into the ATM and trap cash as it is dispensed.

Reproduced with permission from Ombudsman News issue 67/02, February/March 2008, issued by the Financial Services Ombudsman

Bank refuses to refund all of the money taken from a customer's account after he was the victim of a cash machine 'scam'

Mr A tried, unsuccessfully, to withdraw cash from the machine outside a branch of his bank. He said he had entered his details but had then found that the screen failed to function correctly. The machine retained his card and the cash failed to appear, so he went inside the branch to report the problem.

To his alarm, he subsequently discovered that while he had been inside the branch, £300 had been withdrawn from his account. Someone had used his card at a different bank's cash machine in a shopping mall a few minutes' walk away. And a few minutes after that there had been a further withdrawal of £300 from the same cash machine in the shopping mall.

Mr A's bank agreed to refund the second withdrawal of £300. However, it refused to refund the first withdrawal. It said Mr A must have been 'negligent in the care of his card and/or personal identity number ('PIN')'. Mr A then brought the complaint to us.

Complaint upheld
We gathered information from Mr A about his unsuccessful attempt to withdraw money with his card. We also obtained the audit trails from both banks for the cash machines in question.

After examining all the facts, we concluded that Mr A had been the victim of a common scam – often known as the 'Lebanese loop'. A fraudster tampers with a cash machine so that it appears to 'swallow' the customer's card. And having carefully observed the customer using the machine, the fraudster knows the customer's PIN, so can then use the card to take money from the customer's account.

We did not agree with the bank's view that Mr A had been negligent. Applying the provisions of the Banking Code, we upheld his complaint and said the bank should refund both of the £300 withdrawals. We said it should also pay Mr A a further £100 for the distress and inconvenience its mis-handling of the complaint had caused him.

In India, thieves have devised another method by inserting a cocktail stick under the 'OK' button on the PIN pad. The customer enters their PIN, then pushes 'OK'. Nothing happens. When the customer leaves the ATM, the thief returns, retrieves the cocktail stick, pushes 'enter' and continues with the transaction. ATMs that are better designed should return the card automatically if you do not interact with the keypad for 30 seconds.

Longer-term methods of stealing

Stealing the data stored on the card
The thief places a false front over the ATM that conceals additional electronic circuits, so that as you use the ATM, the data on the magnetic strip on the card, together with the PIN, are 'skimmed' or copied. The thieves use this information to produce counterfeit cards for the purpose of conducting fraudulent transactions for use at an ATM that does not support chip cards, such as those outside Europe (or an ATM within Europe that supports fallback). Such devices are also fitted to doors where a bank has placed an ATM inside a protected space. As you swipe your card to gain entry to the lobby containing the ATM, the device records the data on the magnetic strip, although it will not obtain the PIN, because you do not have to key in the PIN to enter the lobby.

The risks that are partly under your control and partly under the control of the bank

There are a number of ways that a thief will try and obtain your PIN. The various techniques are outlined below.

Guessing the PIN

A thief might be able to guess your PIN fairly quickly if you use a sequence of numbers that is easy to guess, such as your date of birth or year of birth, which is the most frequently used sequence of four numbers. For this reason, it is wise to try to remember a sequence of four numbers that are not necessarily linked to such easily obtained biographical information.

Where a PIN is made up of a combination of four numbers, there are only 10,000 possible PINs. If a thief extracts the encrypted form of the PIN from the card with the encryption key, it would take seconds to try all 10,000 possibilities until there is a match.
The banks have included security features that aim to prevent a criminal from guessing the PIN easily: by making it difficult to extract the PIN from the card (whether the PIN is encrypted or not), and by preventing the chip from being used if too many attempts are made to verify the PIN.

Observing or recording a person key in a PIN

A thief will try to obtain your PIN in a number of other ways, as set out below.

Shoulder surfing

Shoulder surfing is where the thief watches you type in the PIN, or they use a device to record you typing in the PIN, such as a miniature hidden camera in the ATM, or by recording the scene with the camera on a mobile telephone. It has been known for thieves to rent flats across from an ATM for the purpose of observing the PIN being used by using binoculars, telephoto lens, or mini-spy-

cameras. In Japan, one method used by thieves was to put miniature cameras in a golf changing room and record the combination used by a player to lock their locker. The thieves assumed, in most cases correctly, that the person used the same number as their PIN.

More recently, thieves have begun to work in supermarkets. They identify older people, watch the PIN being keyed in as the goods are being bought, then distract the victim outside the shop, taking only as long as it takes to steal their wallet or purse. The thief then removes money from ATMs immediately.

False keyboard

Alternatively, a false keyboard is laid over the ATM keyboard. In this way, the false keyboard records the PIN when you carry out a transaction. The false keyboard does not prevent the genuine ATM keyboard from working, it merely records the PIN. A more recent example is to obtain the PIN using a thermal camera to recover the

PIN typed into the keypad, although it is not known if this particular method has been successful.

Smartphones can give away your PIN

When you enter a PIN using your smartphone, the software can identify the PIN. The software records the movements of your face through the camera and records the clicks as you type. It is also possible to work out your PIN by using the gyro and accelerometer.

Obtaining the PIN by tampering with a PIN entry device

A PIN entry device or card reader is the item of hardware into which you insert your card and then key in your PIN to confirm a purchase. It is obviously important to prevent a thief from tampering with these devices; otherwise a thief can open the device, and add an item of hardware to record the account details and PIN. The problem is, even if you inspect the device (as the author does frequently) by picking it up and looking at it from all angles, it will not be obvious whether it has been tampered with, even if a physical seal of some kind has been attached to detect whether it has been opened.

The risks that are under your control
Courier fraud

A more recent variation is called 'courier fraud'. The thief contacts you by telephone (usually an elderly person), usually (but not always) late at night, and tells you that they are the police, bank or the Serious Fraud Office, and tells you that your account has been compromised, which means your card must be replaced. They suggest that you immediately telephone your bank to inform them of this. Once you terminate the conversation, you think you ring your bank, but you don't. The thief has not terminated the telephone call, which means the connection between the thief and you remains live, even if you placed the handset down. This is a peculiarity of the British telephone system – only the person making the call terminates the call, not the person receiving the call. This means you then speak to the thief (or another thief), thinking you are speaking to an employee of your bank. You are requested to key in details on your telephone as if you were interacting with your bank, but the thief knows which keys you press, which means you unwittingly give sufficient information to the thief to steal from your bank account. The thief, masquerading as the bank, assures you that all is well, because they will send a courier around to your home to collect the card immediately. They use a legitimate courier company to collect the card from you, and once the thief has your card in their possession, they proceed to empty your account.

It seems that thieves might have deceived Mr Shojibur Rahman by courier fraud in 2008. Almost £24,000 was removed from his account through cash withdrawals and payment for goods. Mr Rahman took legal action against Barclays Bank, who were held partly to blame for some of the transactions made on his account, because they failed to put a stop to the card when Mr Rahman contacted them. The decisions of the trial judge and Mr Rahman's first appeal before a single judge are available in full in volume 10 (2013) of the *Digital Evidence and Electronic Signature Law Review*.

'Vishing' fraud

'Vishing' is a variation of courier fraud. The thief contacts you over the telephone. They persuade you in the same way as with courier fraud that something is wrong. They use the same technique of getting you to contact your bank (when in fact you speak to an accomplice). They then persuade you to transfer money into an account that might be controlled by the thief, or into an account that they control indirectly. This is called 'vishing', meaning 'verbal phishing' or to steal from you by sounding as if they are advising you in your best interests. The problem with this type of fraud is that the customer authorises the transfer of the money, and because the customer has transferred the money willingly, the bank is naturally reluctant to accept liability.

Chapter 4
The weaknesses of internet banking systems

Online banking enables the customer to interact with what are called the 'back-end' systems operated by banks.

The risks
There are significant risks attached to online banking. There are some fundamental problems that cannot be covered in this book because the technical issues are complex – they include mutual authentication, trust in communication links, and limitations in the way that devices (such as chips on cards) are formatted. You should be aware that thieves can steal money from bank accounts without leaving their own home or country. It is for this reason that you need to be fully prepared for the risks involved in agreeing to the contractual terms imposed by banks.

The banks have begun to take the security of online banking more seriously than previously.

There are a number of different methods by which a thief will attempt to obtain sufficient information to obtain access to an online bank account. A thief might take advantage of technical weaknesses to obtain information when a customer is online, or try and persuade the customer to give up sufficient information over the telephone, by e-mail or by using false web sites to enable them to masquerade as the customer and steal from their account.

Technical methods
Malware
Malicious software is abbreviated to 'malware' in this book, because this is the word that all the experts use. It is a collective noun given to software such as viruses, worms, Trojan horses, backdoors, keystroke loggers, root kits, spyware, pretend anti virus programs, ransomware, droppers and redirectors. The malware of interest in the context of debit and credit cards is designed to enable a third party to obtain data from the computer upon which it has been loaded. Malware is one of the main causes of online bank fraud. For this reason, it is necessary to more fully understand malware.

It is important to appreciate that the banks cannot prevent you from downloading malware on to your computer. Banks also cannot prevent you from running your computer without anti-virus software, although banks invariably include a clause in their contract with you to the effect that you are contractually bound to run anti-virus software on your computer if you use online banking.

How malware is placed on a computer

There are a number of methods that are used to distribute malware. In many instances, the owner or user of the computer will not be aware that malware has been downloaded on to their computer.

The list includes:

'Pay per install' is a service used by criminals, who pay another person to install malware on computers for money. At the time of writing, it costs about £10 to have malware installed on 1,000 random personal computers in North America and Western Europe, and £2 per computer in Asia. The main method of installing malware is through pornography. When a person visits web sites providing free pornography, malware is often downloaded to the computer when images or links are clicked.

When a criminal wishes to target the specific computer of a person with a high net worth, rather than looking for thousands of victims, the main method of getting malware on to the computer is by way of attaching the malware to an e-mail, so that if you click on the attachment, the malware is secretly downloaded onto your computer.

'Drive by download' is where the malware is placed on a respectable web site (which will probably have a security weakness that has not been fixed) without the knowledge of the owner of the web site. Variations involve using social networking sites, so when you visit the web site, your computer downloads the malware without your knowledge. In reverse, if you have the malware on your machine, the software might attach itself to the social networking site to increase the number of computers that download it.

Malware may be offered as an 'app', usually in the form of a free item of software that claims to provide a useful service to the recipient. This is the main method of distributing malware on mobile telephones.

Malware can also be distributed physically, for example by including it on a USB stick. This method is very well known for the purpose of industrial espionage.

What malware is capable of doing when placed on a computer

Malware is usually written either to obtain information, or to cause a computer to do something that furthers the nefarious activities of the people that wrote or purchased it. In the context of banking, malware is designed for the following purposes:

Simple malware is designed to record logon and other data from the computer on which it runs, and sends it to the person controlling it, who will usually sell the information to thieves. Such malware will include a key logger, or key stroke logger, which records all keys pressed on the keyboard; the log is sent to a control server and then scanned for bank log-on credentials (such as passwords, account numbers and such like).

Malware can be designed to do anything that a computer is capable of doing. In addition to recording key strokes, it can record screen shots of the web sites you have visited, conceal that your computer has been compromised, and disable any anti-virus or other defences you have put in place. For instance, the malware can go online and delete all your e-mail. It is also usual for malware, once it is on your computer, to connect to the internet regularly and download more malware in the form of up-dates.

Steal your bank details and authentication information (passwords, etc) for the purpose of fraud.

The characteristics of malware include:

   It is relentless and efficient

   It is difficult to detect and remove

   It is good at preventing security software from deleting it

Methods to try and prevent malware from being installed

The response by the banks

In an attempt to prevent this type of harm, some banks issue customers with a device that generates a different password for each logon. To overcome this additional layer of security, thieves use more sophisticated malware to conduct a 'man-in-the-middle' attack. When this happens, the malware is positioned between you and the bank when you have logged on. Once you have provided all the information to log into your bank account, the malware takes the session over, which enables the thief to instruct the bank to transfer funds from your account.

Some banks use hand held devices to calculate authentication codes for each payment transaction. To get around this type of security mechanism, even more advanced malware can use a different mechanism, called a 'man-in-the-browser' attack. When you have logged on to your bank account, the malware interposes itself in real time between you and the bank. This enables the thief to see and modify any information sent from the bank to you, and from you to the bank.

How you should respond

Keep software up-to-date
All computer software contains errors (often referred to as 'bugs'). Some errors give rise to vulnerabilities that can be used to install malware without the knowledge or consent of the user or owner of the computer. Software vendors regularly provide up-dates or 'patches' when errors have become known. The most important security precaution is by far to keep your computer's software up-to-date at all times.

Install anti-virus software
Using anti-virus software has some benefits, but it is not perfect. Anti-virus software used to detect most known forms of malware, but writing malware is now a business. Malware vendors test their products against the products sold by the anti-virus vendors before using them. This means that most new malware is not detected by anti-virus software at the time malware is used for the first time.

Of particular importance is what is called 'zero-day' or 'zero-hour' threats. This is a term used to describe malware that uses errors in software to be uploaded to computers, where the developer of the software is not aware of the error, and does not have time to provide a fix for the error. Anti-virus products cannot alert the user or owner of a computer to such malware, because they do not know about the software error until they discover the new malware. This means that the anti-virus software might be up-to-date, but it will not notice every item of malware being installed on the computer, although some forms of anti-virus looks for and block suspicious activity by software, such as new software trying to write to system files.

Despite the disadvantages, anti-virus software has a role to play in identifying malware, and you could be considered to be negligent if you do not use anti-virus software, ideally up-dating it every day. However, 'zero-day' or 'zero-hour' threats demonstrate that anti-virus software can still be ineffective. This is important, because banks generally require customers that want to obtain access to their bank account online to have anti-virus software installed on their computer. The logic of the position adopted by the banks is this:

> 1. If Alice has anti-virus software on her computer, and if malware is successfully downloaded on to Alice's computer without being detected by the anti-virus software, and it causes money to be transferred from her bank account without her authority or knowledge, then the bank will probably not hold Alice liable.

> 2. If Bob does not have anti-virus software on his computer, and if the same malware that is not detected by the anti-virus software on Alice's computer is also successfully downloaded to Bob's computer at the same moment in time as it occurs on Alice's machine, and it causes money to be transferred from his bank account without his authority or knowledge, then the bank will probably tell Bob that he is liable.

This illustrates the weakness of the security measures that can be put in place, and shows that the banks offer you a service, knowing that the security is flawed, although you, if you are sufficiently educated, will realise that if you use online banking, you face significant risks.

Personal firewalls can be useful (arguably, they are essential), but some are not well designed or easy to configure properly, which means most people cannot use them effectively.

Using web sites that display a locked padlock or key symbol in the browser
Banks often advise customers to only shop on web sites with a locked padlock or key symbol in the browser. The assumption is that where a web site displays a locked padlock or key symbol, a 'security certificate' protects the site. However, the locked padlock or key symbol is not as safe as claimed.

The locked padlock or key symbol in the browser, together with an address that begins 'https' (also called Secure Socket Layer or SSL), was introduced in an attempt to provide an element of security to you when you viewed web sites. Some browsers will also show a green band to indicate that the web site is 'safe'. It is often asserted that SSL provides a safe connection. However, SSL only provides an encrypted link between your computer and that of the host computer, which is what it is designed to do. It does not prevent:

1. Malware that is running on your computer from intercepting the data entered by you into a web page before it is encrypted by SSL and sent to the bank.

2. Alert you to false web sites and false SSL certificates.

3. Prevent 'man-in-the-middle' or 'man-in-the-browser' attacks, where the criminal impersonates each point in the chain of communication to the satisfaction of you and the bank, which illustrates the problem about ensuring your computer properly authenticates the bank's computer and vice versa.

It is possible for a Trojan horse to be attached to a web browser that modifies web pages, modifies the content of the web page, and includes additional transactions when you are interacting with your online bank account. A locked padlock or key symbol does not stop this form of damage.

Going to the web site of the bank from a bookmark or by typing in the URL

A common method used by thieves to obtain your passwords is by sending phishing e-mails that purport to come from the bank. When you click on the link in the e-mail, it will take you to a web site that looks like your bank's web site, but is actually controlled by the criminal. When you key in all the information required to enter the bank account online, you will have given the criminal all they need to transfer money out of your account. You can help prevent this form of attack by never clicking on a link to your banks web site. It is important to go to the web site directly by typing in the web site address that accompanies the letter you have received from your bank, not by clicking on the link in an e-mail. However, even by doing this, you cannot guarantee that you are on the correct web site of the bank.

Mike O'Connell, a BT worker who has used the internet for a

number of years, found that six separate transactions to a value of £7,450 had been debited from his account at NatWest. They were point of sale transactions. All of the transactions took place on the same day in April 2012.

Mr O'Connell loaded up the NatWest homepage on his computer and checked 'https' was showing in the browser. He then keyed in his 'ID' number, then three random numbers from his PIN and three random numbers from his password. Apparently this was standard practice for NatWest customers logging into their online account. He was then asked for additional information. Because he thought he was on the secure NatWest web site, he entered his PIN, as requested. Two days later the transactions had successfully taken place.

It is reported that the bank suggested that he could have clicked on a phishing e-mail that took him to a false web address, but he said that this could not be correct, because he knew what a phishing e-mail looked like. It appears that the bank also suggested it could have been a malware virus.

Even though Mr O'Connell had virus protection that he up-dated regularly on his computer with a firewall and real-time scanner, which was also regularly updated, it is probable that malware took over the NatWest web site in this instance.

There are some aspects of Mr O'Connell's experience that illustrate the problems with online banking:

1. Based on the account about Mr O'Connell's case, it seems that his session with NatWest was manipulated by a 'man-in-the-middle' attack. Every bank makes it very clear to their customers that the bank will never ask for the full PIN. In this case, based on the facts as reported, Mr O'Connell should have realised something was wrong when the software requested him to input his full PIN.

2. NatWest had, apparently, given Mr O'Connell an overdraft facility that had been gradually extended over time. Mr O'Connell did not request the overdraft facility, but failed to inform NatWest that he did not want the overdraft. The thieves were able to steal because of the overdraft facility. The lesson here is to be diligent and proactive if the bank wants to give you an overdraft that you do not need – thieves will find your overdraft a useful way of stealing from you.

3. Although Mr O'Connell was partly to blame for giving his full PIN to the thieves, nevertheless the bank uses software to identify unusual transactions on the account. That £7,450 was debited from his account via a number of point of sale transactions over the course of a single day should have alerted the bank that something was wrong. In addition, it would have been of interest to know the individual amounts, the time between each transaction, and the geographical distance between each transaction. By analysing such data, it is possible that the bank could be considered to have been partly negligent.

Attempts by the banks to prevent harm by technical means
Using the internet and something else

The most common effective method of detecting and preventing thieves from succeeding in intercepting an online transaction between you and the bank is to include another form of communication between you and the bank, such as a text message or telephone call. When you initiate a transfer, the bank will send a text message to your mobile telephone, requesting you to enter an authorisation code in the browser that is provided in the text message. However, even this method does not prevent the criminals from circumventing the security. They do this by persuading your telephone company to provide them with an extra SIM card so they can use your telephone, perhaps by claiming that the SIM card has failed, so they can impersonate your mobile telephone.

The Chip Authentication Program

The Chip Authentication Program (CAP) is an initiative introduced for using your chip and PIN card to authenticate you and any banking transactions you might make online. You are given a hand held device with a slot for the card, a keypad and a display. You insert your chip and PIN card into the reader to generate a code number, so you can log on, and use the code as a means of authenticating the transaction.

CAP systems are vulnerable to phishing, particularly when a thief uses the 'man-in-the-middle' technique to relay the authentication messages between the chip reader and the bank. A further problem with the CAP protocol is that you have to trust your bank to program their systems properly. A team at the University of Cambridge has found a number of significant problems with the CAP that might cause difficulties in the future.

Transaction Authentication Number

A Transaction Authentication Number (TAN) does a similar job as CAP – it is a password that is only used once – it usually consists of a list of up to 50 numbers printed on a piece of paper. You collect the list from your bank, or the bank sends it to you through the post. A password or PIN might also be used, and can also be sent to you through the post. When you log on to your account, you cannot begin a transaction until you enter a TAN that has not been used. If the bank verifies the TAN, the transaction can be processed, and the TAN cannot be used again. The TAN is vulnerable to a phishing attempt, in the same way as the CAP.

Tricks with graphics

Some banks in Brazil introduced virtual keyboards in an attempt to thwart key loggers. The customer sees a keyboard displayed on the screen and keys in their password using the mouse. The thieves have got around this by getting hold of the parts of the screen next to where the mouse clicks. Banks in Germany have tried to prevent malware from creating a perfect replica of the genuine bank web site by creating complex visual images that incorporate account and transaction data in ways that are difficult to manipulate.

Undermining human imperfections

Social engineering is a term used to describe how humans manipulate other human beings to obtain information. You ought to be aware of social engineering, and there is much more information in the books on the topic as listed in the relevant appendix. The banks provide some information about the various ways that criminals will try to obtain information from you to steal from your account, but it might be argued that the banks do not provide enough information. The bank cannot respond to such attempts by thieves – it is for you to be aware of such attempts and deal with them appropriately.

Impersonating the bank

A well-known method used by a thief who has stolen a debit card is to telephone you and impersonate the bank. The person impersonating the bank tells you that a suspicious transaction has just taken place, and attempts to persuade you to let them know the PIN for the purposes of cancelling the card. There are many variations on this theme, such as 'courier' fraud and 'vishing', which is described in chapter 3.

Intercepting and relaying information

In the case of online banking, the thief might telephone the call centre of a bank and telephone you simultaneously on another telephone line. When the person in the call centre asks for letters from your password, you are not aware that you are giving the answers to the thief, not to the bank. Arguably, if the banks used voice recognition technology, this method would not be as successful.

Diverting your land line

Another method used by thieves is to obtain all the information necessary to divert your land line, then to instruct the bank that your mobile telephone number has changed – obviously, to their own mobile telephone, which then allows the thieves to steal from your bank account, having by-passed your land line and mobile telephone.

This particular method highlights a significant failing by the banks. When an employee of a bank telephones you, it is for the bank to prove to you that they are genuine; but this is not usually what happens. The assumption is that only you must prove who you are. Employees often just say that they are 'the bank', and keep on telling you that 'they are the bank', even when you correctly ask the employee to prove who they are.

The ease of obtaining personal information

There is also the problem, beyond the control of the banks, of how easy it is for thieves to obtain sufficient information about you and your life, and then to persuade the telephone company and other organisations that you have changed your address or diverted your telephone or diverted your postal mail.

Chapter 5
The contract with the bank

The banking relationship is governed by the contract between you and the bank, subject to relevant legislation and any alleged negligence by you or the bank. This chapter considers, at a very high level of generality, the nature of the contract between you and the bank, and its application to the specific issues of the use of bank debit cards and online banking.

It is important to understand that this chapter does not set out the law between the bank and the customer in any detail. The aim of this chapter is to provide you with sufficient information to be able to understand the basic position in contract between you and the bank in the context of the topics covered in this book.

The discussion below is based on the assumption that you are in credit with your bank. Where you are in credit with the bank, the credit balance in the account is a debt owed by the bank to you. You are entitled to have this debt paid on demand. Should you be in debit or overdrawn, then the law is slightly more complex, and it will be prudent to seek advice of a lawyer specialising in banking.

When you are not liable
It will be helpful to set out when you are not liable.

You are not liable for the following:

> Losses that are caused by fraudulent or negligent conduct of employees or agents or the banks, network partners or merchants.

> Losses relating to any part of the method by which you obtain access to your account that is forged, faulty, expired or cancelled.

> Where you are required to use a device or card, any losses that occur before you received the device, card or code, even when the device, card or code is issued a second time.

> Losses caused by the same transaction being incorrectly debited more than once to the same account.

> Losses occurring after you notify the bank that a device or card

has been misused, lost or stolen, of that it has come to your attention that the security of the PIN has been breached.

Losses from transactions that you have not authorised where it is clear that you did not contribute to such a loss.

The Banking Conduct Regime
Previously, the banks in the United Kingdom produced a voluntary code entitled 'The Banking Code'. On 1 November 2009, the Banking Conduct Regime began under the supervision of the Financial Services Authority. The Banking Conduct Regime replaced the provisions of the Banking Code with the exception of loans. More recently, the government split the duties of the Financial Services Authority and introduced two new organisations:

Financial Conduct Authority (FCA), which regulates the financial services industry in the United Kingdom.

Prudential Regulation Authority (PRA), which is now responsible for the prudential regulation and supervision of banks, building societies, credit unions, insurers and major investment firms.

The Payment Services Regulations
The Banking Conduct Regime and the Payment Services Regulations 2009 now govern the banks. Regulation 62 sets out the circumstances in which the customer is liable for losses. The regulation provides that the customer is liable up to a maximum of £50 for any losses incurred where a transaction is not authorised as follows:

1. Where a card is lost or stolen. It is for the bank to prove on a balance of probabilities that the customer contributed to the losses because of their fraud, or by not following the reasonable requirements of the bank, which in turn causes the loss because of the failure of the customer.

2. Where the customer has failed to keep the security features of the card safe. The bank must prove on a balance of probabilities that the customer contributed to the losses by failing to notify the bank within a reasonable time after they became aware of the misuse, loss or theft of a device or card, or the security of the PIN was breached.

The customer is liable for all losses incurred where they act fraudulently, or where they intentionally or are grossly negligent in failing to comply with regulation 57. Regulation 57 requires the customer to use the card in accordance with:

1. the terms and conditions governing its issue and use; and

2. to notify the bank in the agreed manner and without undue delay on becoming aware of the loss, theft, misappropriation or unauthorised use of the card.

The duties of the bank

The bank may be required to pay the customer on demand where the customer is in credit, but this is subject to three restrictions:

1. the balance available in the account is sufficient to cover the order for payment;

2. the instruction is clear; and

3. the authority of the bank to make the payment has not ended.

If a customer disputes a transaction with their bank when they have used a card or online banking, and the bank agrees to repay the customer, the matter ends. Where the bank declines to refund the money, many customers prefer to put the matter before the Financial Ombudsman Service, and failing a resolution in their favour; the tendency is not to take legal action.

From the perspective of the bank, it is necessary to have sufficient evidence of the instructions of the customer. Whether the instructions are received via an ATM, online or over the telephone, what matters is that the customer's instructions are clear (this was not the case in *Shojibur Rahman* v *Barclays Bank PLC*).

Where a bank offers online banking services, and insists on customers using cards to obtain access to their accounts, it is for the bank to ensure it has proper systems and security in place to establish whether the instructions are clear. The topic of this book deals with the issues around this duty, and the reader is referred to the other chapters in this book to understand the complexities relating to the technology used by the banks to conduct banking services today.

The bank relies on evidence in digital format to prove a transaction took place, whether by way of an ATM, point of sale device or online. However, thieves constantly undermine the methods used to authenticate the customer and how the customer agrees to the transaction. For instance, the customer may not have keyed in the PIN, or the thief might have stolen the customers' card and successfully by-passed the correct PIN, or the thief might have been able to by-pass the chip and cause the ATM to undertake a transaction using the magnetic strip. It can be the magnetic strip of the correct card that was stolen, or a cloned card. In such circumstances, the customer's instructions cannot be said to be clear.

The banks insist on customers using the technology, so it is for the bank to have sufficiently robust systems in place to provide satisfactory evidence that the customer is physically at the other end of the ATM, typing on their computer, or in the shop buying an expensive watch.

The duties of the customer

The contract with the bank will be governed by the terms and conditions of the bank, which are changed by the bank from time to time. Generally, the terms are similar across most of the banks, and they all incorporate terms relating to the duty of the customer. A bank will include terms similar or identical to the duties described below.

Duties in relation to the card

The customer has a number of duties:

1. A requirement to do all that the customer can, within reason, to make sure that the card it is kept secure.

2. Not to give anyone else the card or any information about the card that would enable them to use it (for instance, not to store the PIN on a mobile telephone or a personal organiser).

3. To remember the PIN. In some instances, customers are required not to write the PIN down.

4. To destroy the written details of the PIN sent by the bank.

Example reproduced with permission from Ombudsman News issue 68/05, March/April 2008, issued by the Financial Services Ombudsman Consumer held liable for disputed transactions made with her debit card :

Mrs W contacted her bank to complain that, over a three-month period, £9,600 had been withdrawn from her account without her knowledge. The withdrawals had all been made from cash machines, using her debit card and PIN. She did not consider that she should be liable for the transactions and she thought that the bank should have done more to prevent them taking place.

According to Mrs W, her debit card had been taken from her by a Mr C, who had made the disputed withdrawals without her permission and had then refused to give the card back. She said she often suffered from periods of depression and that, during these periods, Mr C 'exercised control' over her. She assumed that he must have obtained her PIN by watching her use the card.

Complaint not upheld
We examined the audit trails for the cash withdrawals made from Mrs W's account during the period in question. These showed that all the withdrawals had been made with Mrs W's genuine card and associated PIN.

It was difficult, from what Mrs W was prepared to tell us, to get to the bottom of exactly how Mr C had obtained Mrs W's debit card in the first place – or why she had not reported this to the bank right away. We also noted that the disputed transactions were interspersed with undisputed transactions, made by Mrs W herself. This did not seem to tie in with her statement that Mr C had refused to give her back the card.

Mrs W had eventually reported her card to the bank as 'lost or stolen', but not until some time after all the disputed withdrawals had been made. Mr C had told the bank that Mrs W had allowed him to use the card and had given him the PIN. But because Mr C was not a party to the complaint, we had no power to question him about that.

After looking carefully at all the evidence, we accepted that Mrs W had not actually made the disputed withdrawals herself.
However, we were unable to conclude that she had not in any way authorised them. We could not fairly say that the bank should be liable for the transactions, and we did not uphold the complaint. However, we reminded Mrs W that our consideration of her complaint did not affect her right to take the matter to court – where witnesses such as Mr C could be compelled to give evidence.

Duties in relation to online banking

The customer has a number of duties:

1. The customer will be required to do all that they reasonably can to make sure that passwords and similar information is kept secret. For example, the customer is usually required not

to record information on a browser or any other hardware or software that would allow anyone using the same equipment to see the data.

2. The bank will probably require the customer to follow the procedures and instructions in any guidance issued by the bank, and to use a smart card and a smart card reader or similar device when obtaining access to an online bank account.

3. Invariably the bank will require the customer to refrain from making changes to any software provided by the bank, and prohibit the customer from permitting a third party from using or copying any software provided to them.

4. The customer will be required to inform the bank immediately they are made aware of any failure, interruption, malfunction, virus or fault when sending and receiving instructions, or if the customer thinks they are subject to fraudulent activities.

5. The bank may require the customer to ensure that any of the equipment used for online banking (computer, modem), complies with certain standards or other requirements.

6. The customer will also be required to check their computer and other devices for malicious software and security up-dates.

Failing to inform the bank of relevant facts

The customer is required by the terms of their contract with the bank to report anything that might have an effect on the account. In an age when the use of technology in banking has changed the way in which customers interact with their accounts, many of the contract terms imposed by banks appear to be reasonable. When a customer follows the conditions set down by their bank, it is possible that they have a better opportunity of protecting themselves. The annual fraud figures produced by Financial Fraud Action UK (previously APACS) demonstrate that the overwhelming majority of transactions by volume are free from fraud.

However, the technology is not perfect. It has been argued by respected technicians that the banks have generally put technology into operation in such a way that there are significant loopholes, and thieves are happy to manipulate them. The problem for the customer is to produce sufficient evidence to the judge to challenge the bank if they dispute a transaction or transactions. The majority of customers are not aware of the technicalities of the banking systems, and are not aware of the various methods that thieves use to by-pass the security mechanisms. Also, it can be argued that some of the requirements set out in the conditions of operating a bank account might be considered to be unfair.

Unfair contract terms

The provisions of the Unfair Terms in Consumer Contracts Regulations 1999 protect consumers against unfair standard terms in contracts with traders. The Regulations provide:

> 1. That where a contractual term has not been individually negotiated, it will be regarded as unfair if it causes a significant imbalance in the parties' rights and obligations to the detriment of the consumer.
>
> 2. In assessing whether a term is unfair, consideration will be given to the nature of services provided, and to all the other terms of the contract.

Taking into account the inherent risks discussed elsewhere in this book relating to the use of the internet, ATMs and point of sale devices, it is arguable whether some of the requirements set out in the terms and conditions of a contract with a bank can be considered to be fair.

For instance, many banks will require the customer not to write down the PIN (which is often the case), and never to record the PIN on or near the card. Recording the PIN on or near the card might be considered to be negligent, but there are two problems.

> 1. The banking industry is well aware that humans have difficulty in remembering passwords and PINs. Many people respond to the difficulty in remembering different passwords and PINs by recording the password or PIN. Many people also use the same PIN for every card in their possession. There is a substantial amount of research to demonstrate that this is a significant problem, and the banks are aware of the research, and if they claim not to be aware of the research, then they are certainly negligent. (The research is set out in detail in Stephen Mason, *Electronic Signatures in Law* (3rd edn, Cambridge University Press, 2012). It appears very odd that the comments made by Ofcom in a report entitled 'Adults' media use and attitudes report 2013' (23 April 2013) paid so little attention to this fact. For this reason, it might well be considered to be unfair for a customer to commit to memory yet another PIN or password.

Chapter 6
Negligence of the bank and the customer

In England & Wales, bank cards, unlike credit cards, are governed by the terms of the contract between the bank and the customer. For instance, where a customer claims cash has been removed from their account by way of an ATM that they are not responsible for, the bank sometimes refuses to refund the money on the basis that the customer was negligent with their card. On occasions, it might be right that the customer has been negligent, but it is for the bank to prove this. However, there is little or no guidance from the courts as to what constitutes the negligent use of bank debit cards, and this chapter will consider the negligence or carelessness of both the bank and the customer.

For a party to be considered to be negligent, it is necessary:

1. To determine what duties the customer has towards the bank, and what duties the bank has towards the customer.

2. To decide whether the customer or the bank failed to comply with the duty.

3. If the duty was breached, it is then necessary to decide whether the failure caused the loss.

At the centre is the standard of care that the customer and the bank have to comply with.

Negligence of the customer
When deciding if a customer is negligent, it is necessary to consider two issues:

1. Whether the customer acted negligently or omitted to do something they should have done, and if so,

2. Whether the loss was the natural result of the customer's negligence or their failure to act.

The use of technology in banking enables thieves to be far more active and efficient in obtaining relevant information (such as the card number, PIN and security code), and to subvert the technology for the purposes of theft. This means that a thief can intervene between the customer and the bank by obtaining the PIN, for instance. The act of the thief (by obtaining the card number, PIN or security code or all of these) might cause the customer to suffer a loss. The problem is that it is usually very difficult for the customer to confront the bank effectively, and to challenge the bank to properly prove with convincing evidence their assertions that the customer was to blame. It is usually the opposite that is true: the bank does not have sufficient evidence to prove the customer was at fault.

Where the intervention of a third party causes a loss

A customer is not negligent where a criminal act for which they are not responsible intervenes between them and any loss they might suffer. A number of relevant issues arise in this respect. These are set out below. They are divided between concerns that are under the control of the bank, and matters that are under the control of the customer.

Where the bank is in control

Where the thief obtains the card, or the data, or the PIN (or all of these) from the customer

A third party can obtain the PIN and the details of the account in the magnetic strip of the card without the knowledge of the customer. A thief can even obtain the original card of the customer by causing the card to be retained in an ATM, together with the PIN. This is the first area of weakness in the technology that the banks make their customers use. The customer cannot be responsible for failing to deal with such risks, because these are risks within the control of the bank. It must be for the bank to prove that the customer was not the subject of such an attack.

The failure of the ATM and back end banking systems

The customer relies on the hardware and software put in place by the bank and any third parties. Even such an innocuous series of transactions involving an ATM might involve an ATM owned by a third party and rented out to another party, the telephone line to the bank may be controlled by yet another party, who may be responsible for the security; a database link might exist between VISA or LINK or another third party, and a facilities management company might be a link in the chain between VISA or LINK and the issuing bank. For this reason, the customer relies on the security, integrity and robust nature of all the systems in place, together with the assessments of the systems, the results of internal audits, external audits, and audits by insurers. None of this information is made available to the customer, so the customer is placed in the position of having to trust the integrity and reliability of these systems, and the ability of the banks to identify and prevent thieves from undermining its ATMs and online banking systems, and from insider fraud taking place.

The duties of the customer where the customer is partly in control
The duty to protect against forgery

With a cheque, the customer is required to take reasonable precautions against forgery. But with a card and a PIN, it is difficult for the customer to prevent a thief from obtaining sufficient information from the legitimate card when they are using different devices to carry out transactions, such as ATMs and terminals in railway stations and restaurants, for instance. The customer is not in a position to take reasonable steps against forgery, unless they never use their card and PIN.

The customer is under a duty to protect the physical card, but they are not in a position to take care of the information associated with the card, such as the card number, security code and the other information stored on the card. A thief can obtain this information very easily, and it cannot be right that a customer is liable when a criminal copies such information when the customer is undertaking a perfectly lawful transaction, such as using the card in a petrol filling station or restaurant.

When using a card remotely, for instance over the telephone or over the internet, the customer must give out the number of the card and the three digit security number on the reverse of the card. The security number is printed on the reverse of the card in an attempt to prove that the card is in the possession of the customer, because only the person in possession of the card can know what information is printed on the reverse.

This 'safety' mechanism is easily bypassed, because a criminal can photocopy the card without the knowledge of the customer, so they will be in possession of all of the information printed or embossed on the front and reverse of the card, and if they then use the card over the telephone, there is no proof that the person conducting the transaction is the customer and rightful holder of the card.

In this respect, a comment by Baron Cleasby made in 1875 in the case of *The Guardians of Halifax Union* v *Wheelwright* has a resonance to the modern world of banking technology as ever it did when he wrote his comments:

> '... a man cannot take advantage of his own wrong, a man cannot complain of the consequences of his own default, against a person who was misled by that default without any fault of his own.'

This means that if the bank insists on using technology that is inadequate or far from perfect, then the bank must take the consequences. The bank cannot take advantage of the weakness in the technology that customers are required to use, such as: the flows of data through a number of third parties; the failure of employees that are responsible for the technology; and the failure to fully control the complex sub-contracting that takes place within the industry.

The bank cannot complain of the consequences of their own default against customers who are misled by those very defaults of technology and the failure to obey operating manuals.

A card can be 'swallowed' by an ATM, and a thief can persuade the customer to think the ATM has taken the card, and subsequently retrieve the card when the customer has left the scene. The thief can then have a cloned version of the card operating in hours on the streets of a city thousands of miles away.

The distinction between the cheque, and the card and a PIN, lies in the manner in which the two items are used and the ease by which a perfect forgery is possible with the card and a PIN. The customer is in more control of writing out a cheque, but the crucial difference between the cheque and the card and the PIN is that the card and PIN can only be considered to be in the relative safe keeping of the customer, and when the card is used, it is exposed to the weaknesses of the technology.

The function of the PIN
Arguably, the PIN combines two functions. Before considering the two functions, consider the requirements of the bank. The bank needs to satisfy itself that:

1. The card is legitimate (this is difficult to achieve, as the reports about fraud demonstrate), and

2. The card is in the possession of the customer to whom it was issued, or a person authorised by the customer to use the card.

If the bank satisfies itself that its computer systems are interacting with the card issued to the customer (which is not always the case), then the computer system requests the purported customer to undertake one further act to confirm they (or a person authorised by them) have physically inserted the card into the ATM or the point of sale terminal, by keying in the correct PIN. Generally, if the computer systems receive positive results from both interactions, then the bank will permit the person at the ATM or the point of sale terminal to undertake whatever activity they are permitted to do within the terms of the mandate.

The first function of a PIN

The first function of the PIN acts as a means of authentication. The PIN purports to demonstrate that the person that keyed in the PIN knew the correct PIN (there are some forms of attack that do not need the correct PIN – any combination of numbers will act to deceive the card issuer that the correct PIN has been keyed in).

The second function of a PIN

Once the computer systems of the bank are satisfied that the card is legitimate and the PIN is the correct PIN of the customer, then the person at the ATM or the point of sale terminal can undertake any activity on the account that is permitted within the mandate and within the limitations of the technology.

The PIN, even though it is offered to the machine before a transaction is effected, acts as a signature to verify a payment or other form of transaction. This means that the presentation of a card to an ATM, and the input of a PIN, is similar to a cheque that is written out by the account holder, signed, and then presented to the cashier at the bank. The customer completes the action necessary to request a payment in advance of the payment being made by the cashier, and then signs the cheque in the presence of the cashier – all before receiving acknowledgment that a transaction has been authorised. This means the PIN is a form of electronic signature.

To summarise: the customer is at the mercy of unknown unknowns. It is the bank that is aware of many of these unknown unknowns because the problems are internal to the bank. However, the banks are also prey to their own unknown unknowns, yet the banking industry rarely acknowledges the weaknesses in their technology.

The duties of the customer where the customer is in control

The customer's contractual duties are discussed in another chapter, but there is an overlap between some of the duties imposed on the customer in the contract with the bank, and whether the customer was negligent in observing the duties. The customer of a bank owes a duty to the bank when writing a cheque to take reasonable and ordinary precautions against forgery. It must also be right that the customer has a duty to take reasonable and ordinary precautions to prevent their card or any of the information relating to the card (especially the PIN) from being stolen or used by a thief.

The PIN

The bank will include a number of duties relating to the PIN in the contract with the customer. The duties will include:

1. To take all reasonable steps to keep the PIN secret at all times.

2. To take every care to stop anyone else using the PIN.

3. To destroy the piece of paper the bank sends with a record of the PIN.

4. Not to write the PIN on the card or anything else usually kept with the card.

A judge will have to decide what the 'reasonable steps' are that a customer must take to keep the PIN secret, and what the customer must do to 'take every care' to prevent anyone else using the PIN. It is unlikely that there will never be any defined set of guidance produced by judges, because the facts in each case are different.

The duty of the customer not to reveal the PIN

It is certain that the customer will be negligent if they tell anybody what the PIN is.

However, if the customer is disabled or not able to use the card and PIN because of their age or some other infirmity, the customer cannot be considered negligent where the PIN is given to a third party that is authorised to act on their behalf. In such circumstances, the bank should be made aware of such an arrangement in advance, and should be told the name of the person with the authority to act for the customer. Where a third party acts on behalf of the customer, the duties that bind the customer will also bind the authorised third party.

Where a customer gives out the PIN to another person, whether it is a family member or a thief, the customer will, depending on the facts, have acted negligently, and will be prevented from claiming that they were not negligent. An example:

> *Reproduced with permission from Ombudsman News issue 68/02, March/April 2008, issued by the Financial Services Ombudsman Consumer held liable for disputed debit card transactions*
>
> Acting as executor of his late wife's estate, Mr M contacted the bank about a number of disputed cash machine withdrawals that had been made from his late wife's savings account.
>
> The withdrawals, totalling over £6,000, had been made with the card that had been issued on the account. And the transactions had all taken place during the two-month period when Mrs M had been seriously ill in hospital, following a stroke.
>
> Mr and Mrs M's grandson, Mr J, had subsequently been convicted for the theft of the money. Mr J no longer had the money, so it was not possible to recover it from him. And the bank refused to refund Mrs M's account as it considered she must have been 'grossly negligent in her care of the card and PIN'.
>
> **Complaint upheld**
> Mr M did not dispute that his grandson had made the withdrawals. The circumstances in which Mr J had obtained the card and PIN were distressing and unusual. He had arrived at his grandparents' home shortly after Mrs M had a stroke. He had then stolen the card and PIN notification while Mr M was preoccupied with attending to his wife and waiting for the ambulance to take her to hospital.
>
> The bank said that, under the terms and conditions of the account, Mrs M was liable for the withdrawals if she had failed to act with

reasonable care. In its view, by keeping her card together with the PIN notification she had failed to act with reasonable care. However, under the Banking Code a customer's liability is limited unless they acted fraudulently or with gross negligence. Clearly, there was no suggestion that Mrs M had acted fraudulently. So the issue we had to decide was whether, in keeping a note of her PIN with the card, Mrs M had been grossly negligent.

Except when Mrs M took her card out of the house in order to withdraw cash, she had always kept it, together with the PIN notification, in a small box. This was hidden in a small cabinet in an upstairs room of the house. The card and PIN would not, therefore, have been accessible to any casual visitor.

It was reasonable to conclude that Mr J had only discovered the whereabouts of the card and PIN because, over time, he had been able to search through the house while visiting his grandparents.

In all the circumstances, we did not consider Mrs M could fairly be said to have acted with gross negligence. We upheld the complaint and said that Mrs M's estate should be compensated by the bank re-working her account (including interest) as though the disputed withdrawals had never been made.

When assessors at the Financial Ombudsman Service consider complaints, reliance is placed on the guidance set out in the *Electronic Funds Transfer Code of Conduct* (as revised by the Australian Securities and Investments Commission's EFT Working Group, and amended from time to time). Although a customer might not be aware of this Code of Conduct, there should not be a difference between what is covered in the Code and the terms and conditions of the bank.

In assessing whether a customer has contributed to losses by writing down the PIN or another other code, the following principles will apply, as set out in the following document: *Banking & Finance Policies and Procedures Manual (Extract dealing with Credit Card Disputes and Electronic Funds Transfer Investigations)* (Financial Ombudsman Service, 2008). These principles will also apply to any device used for online banking:

1. A user may keep a record of the PIN.

2. The PIN should not be written on the card.

3. The customer should make a reasonable attempt to protect the PIN.

4. If the PIN is not reasonably protected, it must not be carried with the card, or kept in such a way that it could be lost or stolen with the card.

Protecting the PIN includes two aspects:

1. Disguising the PIN in a reasonable way.

2. Taking reasonable steps to prevent the PIN from being obtained without authority.

Where a PIN or password is chosen by the customer, it is important to ensure that it is not easy to guess. For this reason, the Financial Ombudsman Service has indicated that a customer will usually be in breach of the principles where the customer decides on a PIN or password that represents their date of birth or is a part of their name that is easy to recognise.

It is worth being aware of the comments of the Financial Ombudsman Service in relation to PINs. In a media release dated 26 November 2008, 'PIN PAIN?', the following advice was offered:

> 'Voluntary Disclosure of PIN – Limit disclosure of your PIN number, even to family members and close associates, as the Financial Ombudsman Service has found that a fair proportion of disputes about authorised transactions involved a family member or someone closely associated with the cardholder. The EFT Code states that the account holder is liable for any unauthorised transactions where the cardholder has voluntarily disclosed their PIN. Any disclosure of your PIN may leave you unprotected and liable for losses.'

Other ways in which a customer might be considered to be negligent

There has not been any case law in England & Wales to provide a list of examples about what might be considered to be negligent, but a number of cases in Germany provide some guidance. The list below is from the German cases, and judges in England & Wales might reach different decisions because of different facts. However, it is possible that customers might be considered to be negligent in the following circumstances:

1. By keeping a written note of the PIN in an address book together with the card.

2. Where the customer places bank statements and the card carelessly into the pocket of a coat or jacket.

3. If the customer leaves their flat for three or four hours and leaves the card and the PIN on the desk in their flat, or if the customer keeps the card and the PIN in a folder.

4. Keeping the card with the PIN (as a four-digit telephone number) together in a solid strong box in a locked sick room in a hospital.

5. Where a purse containing the customer's card is placed in a shopping trolley in a department store.

The customer is also urged to shield the reader of a terminal when they key in their PIN. The value of such shields (when provided) is doubtful, given the wide variety of terminal designs, the location of terminals and how easy it is for others to observe the customer typing in their PIN.

Disguising the PIN or password

In the publication *Banking & Finance Policies and Procedures Manual (Extract dealing with Credit Card Disputes and Electronic Funds Transfer Investigations)*, the Financial Ombudsman Service offer some advice as to what a customer can do to conceal or disguise the PIN or password. They include:

Re-arranging the numerals or letters that the bank has provided, and substituting other numbers, letters or symbols.

Concealing the PIN or password by:

making it appear as another type of number or word, or surrounding the PIN or password with other numerals, letters or symbols

placing the PIN or password in a location or context where it would not be expect to be found, such as on a piece of paper in a cookery book

using a combination of all of these approaches

Assessing how reasonable the disguise of the PIN has been

Where a PIN or password has been disguised, the method used by the customer might not have been effective. The Financial Ombudsman Service has indicated that the attempt to disguise the PIN does not have to be the most reasonable that could have been used. Just because the method of disguising the PIN was not successful, it does not make the attempt to disguise it unreasonable. How reasonable the disguise was will be considered on its merits, and each case must be taken individually.

In considering whether the attempt to disguise was reasonable, an assessment will be made from the point of the reasonable user. The reasonable user is a person:

of average intelligence

who does not have the knowledge and experience of a thief or bank claims officer about the strengths and weaknesses of different types of disguise

who has sufficient, but not specialised, computer skills when it comes to using facilities such as online banking who is aware of widely publicised warnings by their bank and the Ombudsman about unsafe methods to disguise a PIN or password, and would not use such methods unless additional features of disguise were also used in an attempt to disguise a PIN or password

If a PIN or password is disguised in a way that a thief can easily find it, it is more likely that the customer will be considered to be negligent. Examples provided by the Ombudsman include:

1. Recording the PIN as a series of numbers with any of them marked, circled or highlighted to indicate what the PIN is

2. Recording the PIN or password in such a way that it stands out as a PIN or password, for example where the PIN is recorded as a four digit 'telephone number' when all the other telephone numbers are eight digit numbers

3. Recording the PIN or password in isolation from other information

4. Recording the PIN as a birth date, postcode or telephone number without the benefit of a further element of disguise.

Negligence of the bank

There are a variety of ways in which a bank can be considered to be negligent in undertaking its duties towards its customers. In broad terms, it will be necessary to challenge the efficiency of the security mechanisms put in place by the bank. In this respect, the methods used by criminals listed elsewhere in this book will help the customer raise challenges in respect of the efficiency or otherwise of its security systems.

Where an ATM is the regular target of thieves

One interesting possibility is to allege that a bank has been negligent in circumstances where the bank is aware that a particular ATM or number of ATMs are the regular target of thieves. In a programme entitled 'Fraud Squad', which was broadcast on ITV1 on 5 April 2012 between 9 and 10 pm, police officers from the City of London Police and the Dedicated Cheque and Plastic Crime Unit were followed during the course of three cases of criminal gangs from Romania, filmed stealing from ATMs. The police were aware that thieves regularly used one particular ATM owned by Barclays Bank in Portman Square in London to steal money. The images broadcast clearly showed the damage to the ATM. The police officers admitted that this particular ATM was notorious for criminals to use, and a permanent cctv was placed in such a position that the staff in the bank could monitor the ATM at all times. Arguably, if a bank is well aware that a particular ATM or number of ATMs are regularly used by thieves to steal in a similar fashion, the bank could be considered to be negligent for failing to provide sufficient security in place to protect customers that use the machine.

The duties expected of the banks

The book *Banking: Conduct of Business sourcebook* sets out the duties expected of the banks. Additional help can be found in a guide written by the British Bankers' Association, the Building Societies Association and the Payments Council for its members, entitled *Industry Guidance for FSA Banking Conduct of Business Sourcebook* (January 2011). The introduction states that 'Firms regulated by the FSA must also comply with the FSA's Principles for Businesses'. This document makes it clear that the industry accepts that it is necessary to provide customers with proper advice and help. The introduction to section 5 is very interesting:

Section 5: Post sale requirements

5.1 Introduction
Chapter 5 of BCOBS sets out rules relating to the way in which a firm must treat a customer after they enter into a contract for a product or service. Firms must act promptly, fairly and efficiently when providing retail banking services.

The way that firms deal with customers post sale is important in achieving the desired outcomes for Treating Customers Fairly under FSA's Principle 6. In particular firms should have regard to outcome 5:

"Consumers are provided with products that perform as firms have led them to expect, and the associated service is of an acceptable standard and as they have been led to expect."

As per Chapter 2 of BCOBS, all information provided to customers post sale must be fair, clear and not misleading.

The investigation

What is curious is what this document leaves out. It does not require the banks to conduct a fair, efficient, thorough and speedy investigation. It might be argued that a bank has failed to 'act promptly, fairly and efficiently' where:

1. Employees have responded in an aggressive and unhelpful manner to a complaint relating to unauthorised transactions.

2. Where the bank does not investigate a complaint, or does not investigate the complaint with any due diligence.

It will be for the judge to determine, having listened to the evidence, whether a bank has conducted a fair, efficient, thorough and speedy investigation. Some of the factors that should be considered in deciding whether the bank has acted with diligence will include, but not be limited to:

1. How swiftly the bank put a stop on all future transactions after being informed by the customer that they were not responsible for a number of transactions.

2. The speed at which the bank physically inspected any ATM or point of sale terminal.

3. The quality of the technical evidence, and whether the bank made any attempt to balance the technical evidence from their logs relating to the transactions in dispute against the transaction counter on the customer's card.

4. Whether the bank took any steps to secure any relevant cctv recordings and give a copy to the customer.

The security systems

Of more help to the customer in challenging the bank, is in relation to the security systems used by the banks when operating ATMs and online banking. Section 5.9 of the *Industry Guidance for FSA Banking Conduct of Business Sourcebook* sets out the position, as agreed by the banks themselves:

5.9 Account security
To provide a fair and efficient service firms must provide secure and reliable banking systems. Important aspects of this process include having effective systems in place to allow customers to report thefts or losses and making available to customers useful information to help them protect their accounts.

Such information could include:

• how to notify the firm promptly of any changes to the customer's personal information e.g. name, address and contact details;

• the benefits of checking statements and passbooks regularly and alerting the firm to any irregularities;

• how to keep cards, PINs, chequebooks, statements and security details safe; and

• how to alert the firm promptly to the loss of theft of any account details.

If using online banking:

• how to keep the customer's PC secure;

• how to keep passwords and PINS secret;

• the need to treat e-mails from senders claiming to be from the firm with caution and being wary of e-mails or calls asking for personal security details; and

• advising customers how to access internet banking sites by typing the bank or building society's address into the web browser i.e. not using a link in an e-mail.

Firms are encouraged to refer to the relevant rules at BCOBS 5.1.11 and 5.1.12 for details of a firm's and a customer's liabilities for unauthorised payments.

The banks have accepted that they must 'provide secure and reliable banking systems.' Furthermore, the banks also accept that an important part of the process includes 'having effective systems in place to allow customers to report thefts or losses', but not, it seems, a fair, efficient, thorough and speedy investigation.

Chip and PIN technology has had an adverse effect on customers in two significant ways:

1. A card with only a magnetic strip used to rely on the manuscript signature, so it was possible, but probably expensive, to identify forged signatures. This means that where a correct PIN is entered, the bank assume they are dealing with the customer, or a person authorised by the customer.

2. The systems used by the banks are 'one size fit all'. This means a thief can obtain a PIN by observing a low-level transaction (say, a cash withdrawal for £30), and can then use the PIN for a high-level transaction (for instance, to remove as much cash from the account permitted every day).

With a good understanding of the large number of technical vulnerabilities that online banking, ATMs and point of sale devices are prone to, it is arguable whether a bank can be said to have provided 'secure and reliable banking systems'.

Where the bank fails to be certain they are dealing with the customer

A bank is liable to the customer if the customer has not authorised a transaction. This is called the mandate: the bank must have the mandate of the customer to carry out a transaction.

Technical measures used by the banks to identify unusual patterns of use on the account

The banks use a variety of methods increase the probability that it is interacting with the customer when the software in an ATM (or software from a computer or smartphone that is online) is communicating with the back-end system of the bank. The customer is aware of some of these methods: the password and PIN are two examples.

However, the banks also use methods that are hidden from the customer. The aim is to increase the probability the customer is online or at the ATM, not a thief. The mechanisms are normally implemented on the bank's server. Customers are not aware that the bank uses additional authentication mechanisms, and the banks do not reveal what data they use for such tests. However, there is a full list of the methods used by the banks in a document entitled *eID Authentication methods in eFinance and e-Payment services Current practices and Recommendations*. This document was published by the European Union Agency for Network and Information Security Report in 2013, and you can find how to obtain a copy in the appendix of further information.

It can be argued that the bank is negligent where it fails to have proper systems in place to highlight when an unusual activity takes place on the account. In this context, the tests for negligence are:

First, whether the bank has a duty to the customer to ensure only the customer issues instructions (e.g., transfer money between accounts, withdraw money from an ATM) on their account.

Second, if the bank has a duty to the customer, the question is whether the bank failed to comply with the duty.

Finally, if the bank breached their duty, whether the bank's failure caused the loss.

Arguably, the bank has a duty to monitor the account in the electronic age, given the nature of the risks, which are now well-known.

Thieves have begun to manipulate people psychologically (called social engineering) very effectively through courier fraud and vishing. The thieves persuade the customer to provide them with information about their account, including all the security details and, if possible, the PIN. Once a thief thinks they have sufficient information to masquerade as the customer, they will then use the information they have obtained from the customer to steal from their bank account.

An example of how the thieves do this is illustrated by the case of courier fraud involving Mr Shojibur Rahman from 2008. Mr Rahman, a bus driver, had been a customer of Barclays Bank for two or three years. He managed to save £24,400 in a bonus savings account with Barclays Bank, and had £2,300 in his current account. Once the thieves obtained Mr Rahman's card, they used it to withdraw money from an ATM. Taken together, the thieves stole £23,915.76. Part of the theft was to use Mr Rahman's card to buy a Rolex watch from Watches of Switzerland at a cost of £14,420. The thieves could not buy the watch without transferring money between the accounts, and this they did: £20,400 was transferred from the saver account to the current account.

The transfer of funds between accounts
The bank must prove either that it had authority from Mr Rahman to transfer the money, or that Mr Rahman breached his duty because he gave out security information about his account, and this caused the bank to be deceived into believing that it had his authority to make the transfer.

However, the judge hearing the appeal, His Honour Judge Cryan accepted that '[T]he bank did not put before the court any detailed evidence about the security information it sought from the fraudster. It had no record of that transaction, save in general terms.' Here is the problem – the bank did not provide any evidence of the information it required to authenticate Mr Rahman. It was not even certain what method the thief used to authorise the transfer. At trial, the District Judge said in her judgment at paragraph 31 that:

> 'Unfortunately, the defendant has not been able to produce any information as to the precise way in which the transfer was effected. Its records show it was over the telephone but not whether this was by speaking to someone at a call centre or automatically by keying in the sort code, account number, passcode and registration key.'

Given the fact that the bank could not prove that Mr Rahman made the transfer, it is difficult to understand how Mr Rahman can be held to be negligent in such circumstances. Had the bank not transferred the money from the saving account, the thieves could not have gone on to attempt to buy the Rolex watch.

Both the judge at trial and His Honour Judge Cryan dismissed this very important point. On the face of these decisions, it appears that a bank did not have to prove it had Mr Rahman's instructions to transfer the money between his accounts.

This decision is very important, because it affects every person with a bank account in England & Wales. If this decision is not successfully appealed to the Court of Appeal, it is possible that a bank might think it will no longer need to prove their customer gave instructions to transfer money.

Buying the watch
About five hours after obtaining the debit card from Mr Rahman, the thief bought a Rolex watch from Watches of Switzerland for £14,420. Before the thief was able to complete the transaction, they had to answer a number of questions to authenticate themselves – as they impersonated Mr Rahman.

The bank had the burden of proof to prove it was Mr Rahman they were speaking to when buying the watch. The trial judge in her judgment at paragraph 33 discussed the evidence produced by Barclays Bank to the court. An internal report from Barclays shows that the thief was asked the following:

> First, how long the account had been open. The answer was 10 years or something. (The account was in fact opened three years earlier in August 2005).
>
> The second question was where his account holding branch was. This was answered correctly.
>
> The third question was whom he shared the account with. This was answered correctly (i.e. no one).
>
> The fourth question was how long he had been at his current address. The answer was 'all my life' which even the Barclay's report noted was quite vague.

The two answers which were correct, that the account was in his sole name and that the holding branch was King's Cross, may have been read from the debit card itself, which contained the sort code and Mr Rahman's name. There was no other indication that there was any other person named on the account.

The trial judge concluded that it was possible that Mr Rahman gave the thief the information. Mr Rahman did not help himself by lying about the circumstances in which he gave up his card to the thieves, and this aspect of the evidence might have acted to sway the trial judge. However, Barclays demonstrated that their employees had failed to authenticate Mr Rahman conclusively. By its own admission, it seems as if Barclays failed to authenticate the holder of the card effectively, or at all. Given the nature of the evidence, arguably the bank should have been held liable for debiting Mr Rahman's account without authority because it failed to authenticate Mr Rahman.

The decisions of the trial judge and Mr Rahman's first appeal before a single judge are available in full in volume 10 (2013) of the *Digital Evidence and Electronic Signature Law Review*.

Chapter 7
The legal basis for a claim

This book does not explain the technical legal differences between credit cards and debit cards. The aim of the book is to provide a broad outline of the legal issues a customer faces in circumstances where the bank refuses to accept that the customer is responsible for a particular transaction or number of transactions that have been recorded.

The nature of the loss

Banks and their customers are debtors and creditors. Although it is commonplace to speak of 'money in the bank', the cash actually held by a bank belongs to the bank, not its customers. The customers' only assets are their debt claims against the bank (if their accounts are in credit).

If a bank refuses to refund money withdrawn from a bank account, the credit balance constitutes a debt owed by the bank to the customer, and this is the legal basis upon which the customer can take action against the bank. The bank is required to carry out the instructions given to it by the customer. Before the introduction of information technology, disputes mainly centred on cheques, and whether a cheque had been forged or not. The manuscript signature on a cheque could be tested to determine whether it was a forgery.

If legal action is contemplated to recover money from a bank, it is crucial to be aware of the rules relating to which party is required to prove what. When a customer alleges that the bank has debited their account without authority, it is for the bank to prove that the customer, or a person authorised by the customer, carried out the transaction. The bank cannot use as its excuse that the technology is so complex, that it cannot prove that the customer carried out the transaction. The banks introduced the technology, not the customer. The banks require the customer to use its technology. If the technology is so imperfect that it enables thieves to undermine the technology successfully, the banks cannot complain about bringing technical evidence to court when it has to prove its case.

The legal right and the burden of proof

Where the bank relies on the purported electronic signature of the customer (that is the PIN or a combination of password and PIN or any other form of code), they are the party relying on the signature, so the bank has the burden of proof. The bank has to prove that it acted in accordance with the mandate. When dealing with a transaction or series of transactions from an ATM, the bank must prove:

1. Cash in respect of each of the transactions was physically withdrawn from the ATM, or that the transaction described on the statement actually took place.

2. The customer's card was used in the transaction.

3. The customer or a person authorised by them concluded the transaction, or that their carelessness enabled an unauthorised person to do so. Even if the correct PIN was entered into the ATM or point of sale device, it does not follow that the customer or a person authorised by the customer entered the PIN. A perfect forgery remains a forgery. The bank or card issuer requires a PIN to be used, even though the use of a PIN acts to prevent the bank distinguishing a forged signature from a perfect signature.

An Example

Mr Tinklin told his story on the ITV television programme 'Tonight: Cyberwars', which was broadcast on 24 February 2011 at 7:30 pm.

In late August 2010, when Mr Tinklin (a magistrate of thirty years standing) received his credit card statement, two transactions were listed less than a minute apart, recording that two amounts of cash had been taken from an ATM for £300 and £200 against his account. Apparently Mr Tinklin had never used an ATM in all the time he had an account with his bank (79 years). Lloyds TSB told him to destroy his card immediately, which he did. In this way, Mr Tinklin destroyed relevant evidence, which you are not supposed to do. Mr Tinklin then lodged a complaint with the police, but the police informed him that the bank was the victim, which meant his loss would not be recorded.

Mr Tinklin subsequently received a letter from the bank indicated that because the PIN was used, he was responsible for the withdrawals, and therefore he had to pay the bill. By this time, the bank where the ATM transaction had taken place (Barclays Bank – a hundred yards from Mr Tinklin's bank) had already digitally destroyed any relevant cctv.

The bank continued to assert that the chip on the card was read, which meant it must have been his card that was used. Eventually, the bank informed Mr Tinklin the 'code' that it insisted proved chip was read. That code was 90 05. By visiting the Visa Integrated Circuit Card Terminal Specification site, it was possible to determine that the 05 simply meant that the ATM that was used was capable of reading both the chip and the magnetic stripe, and code 90 means 'magnetic stripe read only'. This meant the chip had not been read. Although the bank reluctantly agreed that this was correct, it insisted that his actual card was inserted into the ATM.

However, Mr Tinklin used a hand held device at a restaurant a month before the unauthorised withdrawal took place. This is relevant, because the data sent from the hand held device is not encrypted. As a result, an information receiver can obtain the data, including the PIN that was entered. It might be that a cloned card was used, with the information gleaned from the hand held device.

Mr Tinklin subsequently sent the template letter written by Stephen Mason to Lloyds TSB, and as a result, the bank decided to reimburse him the full amount.

The Payment Services Regulations

The burden of proof as explained above is set out in Regulation 60 of the Payment Services Regulations 2009. The Regulation explicitly sets out what the bank is required to prove:

Evidence on authentication and execution of payment transactions

60.—(1) Where a payment service user—

(a) denies having authorised an executed payment transaction; or

(b) claims that a payment transaction has not been correctly executed,

it is for the payment service provider to prove that the payment transaction was authenticated, accurately recorded, entered in the payment service provider's accounts and not affected by a technical breakdown or some other deficiency.

(2) In paragraph (1) "authenticated" means the use of any procedure by which a payment service provider is able to verify the use of a specific payment instrument, including its personalised security features.

(3) Where a payment service user denies having authorised an executed payment transaction, the use of a payment instrument recorded by the payment service provider is not in itself necessarily

sufficient to prove either that—

(a) the payment transaction was authorised by the payer; or

(b) the payer acted fraudulently or failed with intent or gross negligence to comply with regulation 57.

A 'payment service provider' includes banks and issuers of credit. A 'payment service user' means a natural or legal person making use of a payment service, and a 'payment service' means using a debit card or credit card or online bank account.

This means the bank must produce evidence that:

1. The payment transaction was authenticated. This means that the bank must demonstrate that the following procedures worked properly:

    (a) how it verifies the use of the debit card and ATM or online banking account, and

    (b) how all of the personalised security features (e.g. PIN, password) worked.

2. It was accurately recorded.

3. It was entered in the payment service provider's accounts.

4. It was not affected by a technical breakdown or some other deficiency.

If legal action is taken to recover money that the bank has debited from an account, it will be necessary to take into consideration all the other factors that are discussed elsewhere in the book, such as alleged negligence (of the customer or the bank), the problems with the evidence and what to do when a dispute occurs.

The Conduct of Business sourcebook

The Banking Code was replaced by the *Conduct of Business sourcebook* (BCOBS) in 2009, the terms of which are legally binding on the banks. The bank is required to comply with the terms of BCOBS 5.1.11, which states:

> (1) Where a banking customer denies having authorised a payment, it is for the firm to prove that the payment was authorised.
>
> (2) Where a payment from a banking customer's account was not authorised by the banking customer, a firm must, within a reasonable period, refund the amount of the unauthorised payment to the banking customer and, where applicable, restore the banking customer's account to the state it would have been in had the unauthorised payment not taken place.

Not all banks comply with this requirement, and even when the customer has had unauthorised withdrawals from their account when they are in another country, it might take some time and pressure (such as the customer taking their case to the media), before a bank refunds the money.

A great deal will depend on what is meant by the words 'reasonable time'. Unfortunately, there is no guidance from the courts about what a 'reasonable time' means, because there have not been any cases that have tested this point.

Another or an alternative legal approach

An alternative approach to consider is based on the provisions of the Financial Services and Markets Act 2000, and the Financial Services Authority book *Banking: Conduct of Business sourcebook* (FSA sourcebook). Schedule 5 of the FSA sourcebook is headed 'Rights of action for damages', and provides that if the bank contravenes any of the rules, and the customer suffers loss as a result of the contravention, then the failure to follow the rules may be the subject of action under section 150 of the Financial Services and Markets Act 2000, which is set out below:

> 150 Actions for damages.
>
> (1) A contravention by an authorised person of a rule is actionable at the suit of a private person who suffers loss as a result of

the contravention, subject to the defences and other incidents applying to actions for breach of statutory duty.

(sub-sections (2) – (5) are not replicated)

It will be necessary to show that an 'authorised person' contravened a rule. There is no guidance on what rights exist under this section, but the following examples might come within the meaning of section 150 of the Financial Services and Markets Act 2000:

1. Some customers of some banks face abrupt and sometimes aggressive treatment when trying to communicate with the bank over unauthorised transactions. By taking such an antagonistic approach, the employee is not dealing with the complaint 'fairly and efficiently'.

2. Where the bank fails to investigate a complaint, or does not investigate a complaint with any due diligence.

3. By failing to be open and transparent, which arguably includes a duty to have regard to the customers' lack of knowledge about banking and the systems that banks rely upon, and the vulnerabilities of ATMs and online banking which the bank is aware of, or ought to be aware of.

However, the customer of a bank can only take action in such cases where:

1. a rule has been contravened, and

2. they can demonstrate that they have suffered damage.

If a customer cannot show they have suffered damage, then they do not have a right of action under the provisions of section 150 of the Financial Services and Markets Act 2000.

Chapter 8
Some problems with evidence

Customers often face significant problems when employees of the bank are adamant that responsibility for disputed transactions lies with them. The law requires the bank to prove the customer authorised the transactions in dispute. However, the amount of evidence a bank will wish to produce in court will be minimal. Although the bank should provide all of the relevant evidence, often a bank will only present a small amount of evidence, and it will try to refuse to provide detailed evidence.

Despite the bank being required to prove the customer authorised the disputed transactions, this does not mean that the customer can sit back and wait for the trial, confident that they will be vindicated. The bank will invariably develop a theory of the case that involves the customer having authorised the transactions, or they were negligent in such a way that they become liable for the transactions as if they had authorised the transactions to occur.

For this reason, the customer must also prepare their case from a technical point of view. The customer, if they are the claimant, do not have to prove they did not authorise the transactions in dispute, but they will have to introduce sufficient evidence to show:

1. That there was a reasonable possibility that a thief was responsible for the transactions in some way.

2. If it is not obvious how the thief could have effected the transactions, then it will be necessary to bring sufficient evidence before the judge to show that the customer was not responsible for the transactions in dispute.

If a customer has no other option other than to take legal action to recover their money, it will be necessary to ensure they can put sufficient evidence before the judge to demonstrate the bank must be wrong or mistaken. Below is a list of arguments that might be introduced by the bank. The list is not exhaustive.

Common indications
The bank might argue that the transactions that are disputed do not show any 'common indications' that the transactions were caused

by a thief. For instance, a customer might only use their card to withdraw cash from their account perhaps five or six times using an ATM on different days over a month for small amounts (varying between £20 and perhaps £50 or so). The number of transactions will vary each month, as will the amount withdrawn, but generally there will be a pattern: low value on different days throughout the month, mainly but not entirely during the day. When a thief has obtained access to the account in some way, the pattern will suddenly change. Money will generally be taken out of ATMs fairly quickly, in a short period of time, and the amount of money withdrawn will be substantially higher than normal, and probably will also be removed late at night. The total amount withdrawn or transferred by the thief will vary. With the card in their possession, the thief can use it as if they are the customer, assuming they have found out or can bypass the PIN.

There is a significant problem with the way the banks have developed cards. They have created what they think is a very useful item of software on the card when it connects to the ATM. The software permits the customer to interrogate the account to find out the balance in the account. When a thief obtains the card, the software permits the thief to interrogate the account in the same way. Once the thief knows how much money is in the account, they can then decide how to take the money out of the account. The thief is helped if the bank's security systems are so weak that the change in use is not noticed.

The banks will often argue that changes in how the account has been used do not indicate any 'common indications' that a thief is responsible for the transaction in dispute. There are two aspects to their argument that merit attention.

First, it is implied that the bank thinks the customer has deliberately authorised the transactions to make it look as if a thief has obtained the money, and the customer is making a fraudulent claim. This is an odd argument. That is, based on past experience, the bank expects thieves to behave in a certain way. The bank usually asserts without providing any evidence that the transactions do not match their expectation of thieves. As a consequence, the bank argues that it is the customer that is perpetrating the fraud.

Second, the bank might look at previous claims in detail. By taking this approach, it might be possible for the bank to determine with confidence whether the customer was perpetrating a fraud. Statistical models could be used to find 'common indications', but it is not certain that they have such statistical models.

Security certification

Manufacturers of smart cards have obtained certificates relating to security through such schemes as Information Technology Security Evaluation Criteria (ITSEC) and Common Criteria. The purpose of paying to obtain such certificates is to be able to make claims about the security of the card.

The ITSEC scheme

The ITSEC scheme, which is no longer as active as it once was, assesses a document prepared by the organisation that wants a product to be evaluated. In general terms, the document submitted to ITSEC describes what the product is designed to do, the situation in which it is intended to operate in, the risks the product is likely to encounter, and the mechanism by which the product acts to protect against the risks. It is for ITSEC to determine whether the claims are substantiated. Only the risks identified by the applicant are tested. A product is given one of seven levels from E0 (no formal assurance) to E6 (the highest level of confidence). Each level represents increasing levels of confidence. The assessment and granting of a position on the E scale is a judgment that a certain level of confidence has been met. It is not a measure of the strength of the security in place.

It is important to realize that the organisation submitting the product for evaluation sets out the criteria by which it will be evaluated. In all probability, the party submitting the product for evaluation will not have included the risks associated with the use of the product by the customer. The evaluation includes an assessment of:

1. the confidence to be placed in whether the security features are the correct ones, and

2. how effective the security features work.

This means that a security mechanism might be applied correctly, but they will not be effective unless they are appropriate for the purpose for which they have been designed. In this respect, it is necessary to know:

1. Why a particular security function is necessary.

2. What security is actually in place.

3. How the security is provided.

It does not follow that if a product has a high E level, that the product will provide a high level of security.

Common Criteria

The 'Common Criteria for Information Technology Security Evaluation' and 'Common Methodology for Information Security Evaluation' comprise the technical basis for an international agreement called the 'Common Criteria Recognition Agreement'. The manufacturer submits their product to an independent licensed laboratory for an assessment of the product. The way a product is evaluated is similar to the way ITSEC undertakes such assessments.

If a judge is not aware of security certification and the problems listed above (and to be fair, why should they be?), it is imperative that the customer ensures the judge is alerted to this issue.

There is no evidence of chip and PIN being subject to attack

The argument that there is no evidence of chip and PIN being subject to attack rests on the fallacy that because there is no published evidence that a chip and pin cards have been cloned, it can be inferred that such cards have not been cloned. But if criminals have succeeded in cloning chip and PIN cards, it is in their interests to do their best to conceal the fact. Likewise, it is in the interests of the banks, in attempting to reduce their exposure to loss from fraudulent transactions, not to attribute any incident to the cloning of a chip and PIN card if any other explanation can be put forward. Accusations that a customer has acted fraudulently or has been careless can always be advanced, and it is always in the interest of the banks to suggest them as explanations in preference to cloning, because they transfer the loss to the customer, while cloning leaves the loss with the banks. The banks do not know whether criminals have succeeded in cloning such cards: or if they do, they have not made such knowledge public. This proposition amounts to no more than an assertion of the ignorance of the organisation or person making the assertion, and provides no evidence from which anything can be inferred about whether or not chip and PIN cards can be cloned.

Finally, bear in mind a point that APACS itself makes in a document that is no longer available, but the observations remain valid. The comment below is taken from *PIN Administration Policy* (APACS, v1.2, January 2004) page 11:

> '2.1 Security Objectives
>
> The following basic principles that should govern the PIN Management process are adapted from [ISO 9564]:
>
> Assurance
> It shall be possible to prove the security of the PIN Administration process.
>
> *The PIN Administration process must not only be secure, but also be demonstrably secure. If PIN Security is publicly challenged, either in the media or in a court of law, it must be possible to respond to such a challenge and for the response to be supported with evidence. Furthermore, the use of that evidence in the public domain must not in itself compromise security.'*

The presumption the computers are in order

In England and Wales, there is a common law presumption that includes computers by implication (or more accurately, digital data). The formulation of the presumption reads: 'In the absence of evidence to the contrary, the courts will presume that mechanical instruments were in order at the material time'. The problem with this presumption is that software written by human beings has always been – and continues to be – subject to errors (as described in detail in *Electronic Evidence*, chapter 5). This means it is essential to ensure the judge and the lawyers understand that software is prone error or manipulation, and you cannot necessarily rely on such evidence, regardless of the presumption.

Chapter 9
Handling a dispute at the early stages

When you realise that you have had cash withdrawn from an ATM, or you check your statement to discover a number of transactions you are certain you neither authorised nor were responsible for, you must contact the bank immediately. Banks prefer customers to contact them over the telephone, and it is important to think about following some simple steps:

1. During a telephone call, always ask the name of the person that is speaking to you, and if they will not give you their full name, ask for the full name of the call centre they are working for.

2. Take notes of the details of the conversation, to include time and date.

3. Follow up any communication with a letter, sent by recorded delivery.

In this part, you are taken through the possible mechanisms that a bank has put in place to deal with potential theft and fraud.

Contacting your bank
The bank has a dedicated telephone number to report transactions that might be fraudulent. You should make every effort to ring the dedicated number immediately, wherever you are in the world, at whatever time you discover the problem.

It might be that you are taken through the problem very quickly, and after you have explained what has occurred, the employee you have spoken to will have resolved the matter swiftly. However, sometimes you might feel that the bank fails to respond effectively, and might even, in your opinion, be abusive and unhelpful. When you have cause to ring your bank in such circumstances, clearly you will probably be under a great deal of stress, but it is essential to try and keep calm and to be polite to the person working for the bank. This is a counsel of perfection, but far more might be gained by trying to stay calm, rather than taking a high minded approach to the employee on the other end of the telephone. Consider the following points:

1. It might help to understand the position the call centre employees find themselves in. They might not even be an employee of the bank.

2. The employee you speak to will probably not have the knowledge or the authority to provide you with an authoritative statement about the actual process or technology.

3. The person you speak to can only make a decision if it is on the check list they have on their screen. This means it is important to make the complaint in a way that fits in with their check list (which you cannot see, which makes asking questions an art rather than a science.)

4. Their supervisor has no or few additional powers. However, they do have a slightly wider range of available processes they can call upon. It is useful to be aware that the main job of the supervisor is to keep the call-centre workflow moving smoothly, rather than a focus on customer service, which is for their team members.

5. The team manager will have a slightly higher financial write-off, but they will not have any more ability to make decisions.

Preserving the evidence
Turn to the relevant appendix for a list of things you should consider doing immediately.

The investigation
The bank should cancel your card immediately, and an employee will investigate your case, but your case will be added to the queue of cases that must be investigated. The employee whose task it is to investigate cases of fraud will follow a set of scripts, in the same way as employees in call centres are required to. The script is designed to quickly identify those cases with a common explanation to explain what happened, leading to a swift resolution in the majority of cases.

An investigator might spend up to thirty minutes reviewing your case, and they will have access to several online bank systems from which they can review technical data concerning your account. The systems to which fraud investigators have access do not always have all the details necessary to reach a decision, and often the technical data is provided in a simplified form for investigators who do not have the technical or legal knowledge that would necessarily help them to reach a fair conclusion from the evidence that they gather. As a result, mistakes can happen, such as if the system incorrectly muddles up chip transactions and magnetic strip transactions, as seem to have occurred in the case of Jane Badger.

In March 2008, Jane took some cash out of her bank account and noticed that a direct debit in the sum of £772.24 was taken from her account, payable to Egg credit card. Jane disputed this transaction. When speaking to Jane, an employee at Egg told her that they had reset her password on the internet, because she had not been online for 14-15 months. Jane had not used the online facility. Jane was informed that the direct debit payment was to pay for three cash withdrawals from a cash machine in Burton on Trent. These were £250 on the 19 January 2007, £280 on the 21 January 2007, and £200 on the 30 January 2007. Jane did not make these withdrawals.

On 7 March 2007 Jane reported the matter to the police. On 4 April 2007, Jane was arrested at home at 08:20am, and on 13 August, she was charged with fraud by false representation under section 2 of the Fraud Act 2006. She was also suspended from her police job.

On 13 November 2007, Jane's barrister informed her in court that Egg gave the prosecution a witness statement in which an employee of Egg, Mr Craig Homer, made a statement on 28 August in which he stated that he made an error in the evidence against Jane. There was also a statement by a Mr Matthew Williams from Egg, stating that he had looked at the authorization report, and there was a transaction noted that was not clear, and he could offer no explanation for the transaction.

Jane entered a plea of not guilty. Jane subsequently appeared in the Crown Court in Birmingham on 1 February 2008 before Her Honour Judge Chapman. The prosecution offered no evidence against her, and the judge entered verdicts of not guilty in her favour.

If a decision is not reached fairly quickly by following the scripts, then the matter will go to a senior investigator, or the Head of the Technical Investigations Team or the Fraud Investigators and Internet Banking Help Desk.

The bank may refund the amount in dispute quickly, but the decision might be reversed later. This is because the first investigation might conclude that you should be refunded, but after a review a week or so later, a more senior investigator might reach a different conclusion. You should receive a confirmation in writing that your case is closed.

Chapter 10
What to do when disputes occur

The reporting process
When you report a theft to the bank by, the bank decides whether to tell the police. Each police force has a single point of contact (SPOC) that the banks respond to, and if the bank makes a report, it is then for individual chief officers to decide whether the allegation is investigated.

Guidance has been issued to the police and banks, and is included in the Home Office Counting Rules for Recorded Crime. This is a public document and the web site address is provided in the appendix. The complaints procedure is also provided as an annex to various annual reports issued by the LINK Consumer Committee. The web sites for each of these are listed in the appendix.

Where the account holder is the victim (that is, you suffer the financial loss) you are required to report this to the national fraud reporting centre, not to the police. This change took place on 1 April 2013. It will be for the National Fraud Authority to decide whether the police will investigate your complaint.

If the bank decides that you were responsible for the withdrawal (or somebody authorised by you, or you were negligent), then the bank will not reimburse you.

The reaction of the bank

When a customer complains to a bank about unauthorised withdrawals, some banks act with commendable speed and within the law. Regulation 61 of the Payment Services Directive and Payment Services Regulations 2009 sets out the legal position. Subject to Regulations 59 and 60, the bank must immediately refund the amount of the unauthorised payment transaction, and where applicable, restore the account to the state it would have been in had the unauthorised payment transaction not taken place. Unfortunately, there are a number of banks that do not comply with this requirement, and undertake what they call an 'investigation', only to inform you that you carried out the withdrawal. You then have to gather evidence to prove you were not responsible for the transaction.

The police

If the bank will not reimburse you, you can then complain to the police, but all the police will probably do is give you a crime report number, and refuse to take any further action. The police do not tend to take action because of

1. The high number of cases reported.
2. The time it takes to investigate.
3. The expense of investigating.
4. The expertise necessary to follow up such a complaint.
5. The apparent low importance attached to such crimes.

Complaining to the Financial Ombudsman Service

In circumstances where you fail to convince the bank to reimburse the money stolen, it may be necessary to contemplate what further action to take in an attempt to have the money refunded. Before taking legal action, it is necessary to demonstrate to a judge that the parties have tried to reach a settlement. For this reason (and because it is free), it is worth considering making a complaint to the Financial Ombudsman Service.

Before making a complaint, it is necessary to complain to the bank. They will have eight weeks to investigate and consider the complaint. The Financial Ombudsman Service will not investigate the complaint until the initial eight week period has lapsed. The Financial Ombudsman Service web site provides the forms and guidance necessary to initiate a complaint. It is important to be aware that a complaint must be submitted within the time set out by the Financial Ombudsman Service. There is a consumer factsheet available entitled 'How we deal with your case' which is available on the Ombudsman web site, and the document entitled *Banking & Finance Policies and Procedures Manual (Extract dealing with Credit Card Disputes and Electronic Funds Transfer Investigations)* (Financial Ombudsman Service, 2008) sets out the general approach taken to an investigations by the Financial Ombudsman Service.

It does not follow that the Financial Ombudsman Service assess or tests the evidence provided by the banks to the same extent that you would expect to occur in a court. This means that complaining to the Financial Ombudsman Service does not necessarily provide adequate protection for bank customers with disputed transactions.

In addition, the Financial Ombudsman Service might employ ex-bank employees to undertake this work. From the perspective of natural justice, it seems odd that a previous employee of a bank should be paid to adjudicate on complaints made by customers against banks.

Taking legal action

If an application to the Financial Ombudsman Service fails, then you will have to consider taking legal action against your bank. Litigation is often an exhausting process, both financially and personally (causing both physical and mental stress), and this option is best considered after careful consideration of the amount in dispute and the strength of the evidence. If every attempt has been made to have the dispute properly considered, that is, based on the evidence and a proper testing of the evidence, and decisions continue to be found in favour of the bank, then legal action is probably the only option available to you where you are certain that you not responsible for the disputed transactions.

The legal basis for taking legal action

This topic is dealt in detail elsewhere in this book.

Time limit on taking legal action

It is important to be aware that legal action must begin within certain time limits. The time limit depends on the type of legal action. It is necessary to ensure that any legal action that is contemplated is within the time limit.

Before applying to the court

The court will expect the party that begins legal action to have attempted to settle the claim before initiating legal action. In certain circumstances, failure to do so may mean the court might decide that the claimant does not get their costs if they win, and might even be ordered to pay the other party's costs. This means it is important to try to resolve the dispute before taking legal action. If this fails, it is helpful to consider making a complaint to the Financial Ombudsman Service. Even after going through the process of negotiating with the bank and complaining to the Financial Ombudsman Service, a mediation officer appointed by the court is available to offer to reach a settlement before a trial.

Obtaining legal advice and representation

In general terms, the law relating to disputes discussed in this book is straightforward. Assuming you are not in debt and money has been withdrawn or transferred from your account without your authority, the bank is liable to you. The bank must prove that you authorised the transaction.

The law is usually not an issue. The evidence is complex. It is necessary to be familiar with the complexities of the way banks deal with ATMs, point of sale devices and internet banking. It is also necessary to have the help of an expert witness that is familiar with banks and banking systems.

In addition, although legal proceedings for small claims appears to be simple, if you begin legal action without advice or help or any legal representation, then you may find yourself at a serious disadvantage when the bank employs a solicitor and barrister to defend the case. For instance, there are a number of procedural steps that take place within strict time limits, and failure to adhere to these time limits can mean that the case is dismissed, or the person taking legal action misses an important opportunity to force the defendant to produce evidence that it otherwise ought to have produced.

Before taking legal action, it is advisable to seek the help of a lawyer. However, when finding a suitable lawyer, it is essential to consider obtaining answers to some or all of the questions posed in the appendix.

The discussion that follows is a general guide to the small claims procedure. The aim is to only provide an outline of the procedure, together with the issues that a litigant in person ought to consider. The information set out below does not discuss the topic exhaustively, and you are encouraged to consider consulting the web sites and books listed in the appendix for more detailed information.

Terms used in this section

The person making the claim is called the claimant

A claimant or defendant who is not represented by a lawyer is called a litigant in person

The person or organisation defending the claim is called the defendant

To start a case, it is necessary to fill in a claim form

When the claimant begins a case, the defendant is notified of the legal action by what is called 'service', and the court sends the papers to the defendant

If the court decides the claimant is right, and finds against the defendant, the claimant, if the defendant fails to pay, can apply to the court for an order to make the defendant pay – this is called enforcement proceedings

Where to begin legal action

Legal action can be started in any county court. It is better to make an application to the nearest court. If you move to another part of the country after the legal action is begun, you need to request the court in writing to transfer the proceedings to your nearest country court.

Facilities for disabled people

If you are disabled, you will need to contact the court to explain the nature of your disability, so the court can offer appropriate advice.

Beginning the claim

The legal action begins with the claimant filling out claim form N1. Claim forms are available online, and physical copies can be obtained from a county court. Guidance on the information to include and how to fill in the part headed 'Particulars of Claim' are set out in the appendix, and the court services also provide a leaflet that offers more help, entitled 'How do I make a court claim?'.

Court costs

Once legal action begins, the court will require you to pay a fee when you hand in the claim form. Additional court fees will have to be paid at different stages during the legal process. In certain circumstances, the fees may be waived or reduced by the court, for example, because you receive benefits, or have a low annual income, or will suffer financial hardship.

Handing the claim form to the court

It is necessary to take the original form that you have filled in, together with a copy of the form, to the court. It is wise to retain a copy. When handing in the form, the fee must be paid to the court. When the court has received and issued the claim, it will send you a 'Notice of Issue'. The court will also send a copy of the claim to the defendant. The defendant can admit, defend or admit part of the claim.

The bank does not defend the claim

If the bank does not defend the claim, it must pay the money in dispute. If the bank fails to make the payment, you will need to ask the court to issue an order to the bank to make the payment.

The bank defends the claim

If the bank defends the claim, in whole or in part, then it must respond within 14 days of the date it was served by the court. The bank can send (called 'filing') an acknowledgment of service, or a defence. If the bank files an acknowledgment of service, it will give them extra time to prepare the defence. In which case, the time for filing a defence increased from 14 days to 28 days from the date of service of the claim. Where the bank defends the claim, it will probably have asked a lawyer to prepare a defence to the particulars of claim.

When the court receives the acknowledgment of service, you will be sent a notice that acknowledgment of service has been filed, and when the defence has been filed, the court will send you a copy. For more information, see the leaflet 'The defendant disputes all or part of my claim'.

The allocation questionnaire

If a claim is defended, a judge is required to make sure that the case is properly prepared and proceeds swiftly to a final hearing or a trial. The court calls this 'judicial case management'. A judge will allocate the case to one of three tracks. The three tracks are:

- Small claims track
- Fast track
- Multi-track

Each type of claim is handled in a different way by the court. In deciding which track to allocate the claim, the judge will take account of the amount of money claimed, the complexity of the case, and whether an expert report is necessary. The judge will make this decision without hearing the parties in the case. Unfortunately, in disputes relating to ATMs, point of sale devices and internet banking, judges tend to make these decisions without understanding the complex nature of the electronic evidence. Often, this acts as a significant disadvantage to the claimant, especially if the claimant is a litigant in person. This is because such cases include a great deal of complex evidence, and it will be necessary to have evidence from experts in banking systems to provide explanations about how the systems work, and how the systems fail. It is for this reason that it is very important to fill in the allocation questionnaire.

You must also ensure that you provide good reasons why it is necessary to have an expert witness, because the judge must give permission for an expert to give evidence.

As a rough guide, if the amount in dispute is £5,000 or less, the claim will be allocated to the small claims track. If the case is more complex, the case will probably be allocated to the fast track or multi-track.

Finally, it is essential for a litigant in person to be aware of the relevant Civil Procedure Rules and Practice Directions, all of which are available online:

> Small claims are dealt with Civil Procedural Rule Part 27 'The Small Claims Track' (CPR 27) and Practice Direction 27, which supplements CPR 27
>
> Fast track claims are dealt with Civil Procedural Rule Part 28 'The Fast Claims Track' (CPR 28) and Practice Direction 28, which supplements CPR 28
>
> Multi-track claims are dealt with Civil Procedural Rule Part 29 'The Multi-Track' (CPR 29) and Practice Direction 29, which supplements CPR 29

The allocation of track and the effect on costs

If you are a litigant in person, it is crucial to understand that your liability to pay the costs of the other side will be affected by which track the case has been allocated. Where a case has been allocated to the small claims track, with some exceptions, neither party pays the other party's costs, fees and expenses, including those relating to an appeal. However, the procedural rules also permit the judge to order one party to pay the other side's costs in certain circumstances, and when you consider taking legal action to resolve a dispute, you must pay careful consideration to the possibility that you might be ordered to pay for some of the costs of the other party, in accordance with the provisions of CPR 27.14 (these provisions are too detailed for this book to consider them).

When the questionnaire is returned

When the questionnaires are returned to the court, or if they have not been returned, and the time of their return has passed, the case file will be given to a procedural judge. If the questionnaires have been returned, the judge will use the information provided in the questionnaires to help decide which track to allocate the case to. The decision of the judge is sent to the parties in the form of an order called a 'notice of allocation'. The notice will tell the parties which track the claim has been allocated to, and what the parties must do to prepare the case for trial or the final hearing (this is called 'directions').

If the case is allocated to a track that is different to the one that either party was expecting, the judge will give their reasons for making a different decision.

If you are a litigant in person, a change of track from small claims to fast track or multi-track has significant implications regarding your exposure to being made liable to pay the costs of the bank if you do not succeed at trial. This is an issue of the utmost significance. It cannot be emphasised too much that if a litigant in person anticipated the case will be allocated the small claims track, but it is allocated any other track, they can expect to face the possibility of paying up to and over £40,000 costs to the other side if they the case goes against them. This figure is not a hypothetical amount. In one ATM case (*Job v Halifax*, 2009), the costs requested by the bank were just under £50,000. Although the judge did not order the entire amount to be paid by the claimant, the claimant entered into an agreement to pay just over one fifth of this figure.

Where a judge decides that the small claims track is not suitable, the claimant, if they are a litigant in person, ought to consider taking legal advice to determine whether they can challenge this decision on the basis that it might leave them with no option other than to withdraw from the case, for fear of being exposed to the possibility of paying the costs of the bank if they do not succeed.

If the questionnaire is not returned by the due date

The court administrators will refer the case file to the procedural judge immediately after the time for returning the questionnaires has expired. This will occur whether only one or neither of the questionnaires has been returned. At this stage, the judge can decide to allocate the case to a track anyway, or send an order to the party that has not submitted the questionnaire to file a completed questionnaire within a set number of days.

If the claimant fails to comply with such an order, the particulars of claim might be struck out, and if the bank fails to return the questionnaire, the defence might be struck out. This means that you cannot proceed with your claim, or the bank cannot proceed with the defence, because the documents will be deleted from the record and cannot be used.

Alternatively, the judge can order the parties to attend to explain why they did not comply with the court's request. If this happens, the judge may order the party that has not handed the questionnaire in to pay the other party's costs of attending that hearing. The judge might use this hearing to ask for the information necessary to allocate the case.

The hearing date

It is normal for the judge to include the time, date and place of the hearing or trial in the notice of allocation that is sent to each party. If you cannot attend the court on the date set by the judge, you must inform the court immediately (by telephone and post), and apply for the judge to decide on another date. The judge will only agree if there is a good reason.

The notice of allocation will also include an estimate of the time allocated to the trial. The time allocated to a trial is important, because a judge will usually give a short time for a claim involving a small amount of money.

However, as has been pointed out throughout this book, banking disputes are complex, because of the nature of the banking systems. It is for this reason that although the amount in dispute might be small, the questions relating to proof are significant. This means that if a judge only allocates an hour or so for the trial, this must be challenged if the parties know it will take longer. It is important to get the advice of any expert witness that might be called to give evidence. It is usual for a trial relating to banking to take at least one day, depending on the issues to be tried.

The lead up to the hearing

When the judge issues the notice of allocation, they will also include a direction that each party must, at least 14 days before the date fixed for the final hearing, file and serve on the other party copies of all documents (including any expert report) on which they intend to rely at the hearing.

This action of exchanging documents is also called 'disclosure'. This is the most important part of the proceedings before trial.

It is at this stage that each side gives the other side every document on which they intend to rely. This is particularly relevant to the bank, because they will invariably only disclose those documents they want to, and they will probably not produce all the documents that will be necessary to provide the evidential foundation for the evidence upon which they rely.

It cannot be emphasised too much that you must have a list of documents that the bank should be made to disclose, which is why a list of the questions to ask a bank and a list of the types of document that you need to see is provided as an appendix. It is highly probable that you will have to apply to the court to require the bank to disclose many more documents. If you fail to make this request, the trial will take place without a great deal of relevant evidence being put before the judge. This also means that you will not be in a position to challenge the authenticity, integrity and trustworthiness of the ATM and banking system, which might mean you will not be able to effectively test the assertions by the bank that the evidence can be trusted.

If you are forced to ask the judge to order the bank to provide more evidence, because the bank has refused to provide the additional evidence you have asked for, it will be necessary to apply to the judge to issue an order to the bank to provide the documents. Any request must give the reasons for wanting the bank to disclose the evidence. Bearing in mind a dispute about an ATM, point of sale device on online banking is far more complex than the vast majority of cases brought before the civil courts, it is important to ensure the judge understands this. It is also very important to ensure that if it is necessary to make a request for specific disclosure, and that the list of documents requested:

1. Are set out clearly.

2. A reason for asking for the document is given.

3. The nature of the document requested is very clear.

If none of the information set out above is provided, then a judge will not be in a position to make an order. It is unlikely that such a list can be drawn up without the help, advice and guidance of somebody that knows banking systems.

Where you request further evidence from the bank, it is necessary to be aware that the bank will invariably try not to produce more evidence, and it will refer to what is called the 'overriding objective', which forms paragraph 1.1 of the Civil Procedure Rules. This reads as follows:

(1) These Rules are a new procedural code with the overriding objective of enabling the court to deal with cases justly.

(2) Dealing with a case justly includes, so far as is practicable –

(a) ensuring that the parties are on an equal footing;

(b) saving expense;

(c) dealing with the case in ways which are proportionate –

(i) to the amount of money involved;

(ii) to the importance of the case;

(iii) to the complexity of the issues; and

(iv) to the financial position of each party;

(d) ensuring that it is dealt with expeditiously and fairly; and

(e) allotting to it an appropriate share of the court's resources, while taking into account the need to allot resources to other cases.

There are many aspects to the overriding objective, but the bank, or the lawyers for the bank, will usually pick out items (2)(b) and (c)(i) in isolation, and argue that any requests for additional documents will be contrary to the need to keep costs down. The lawyers will rarely address the most significant issue: the complexity of the case. It is for this reason that whenever additional documents are requested from the bank, it is essential for you to:

1. Have a good reason for asking for them.

2. Explain to the judge that modern banking systems are now so complex, that much of the technical evidence is required by both parties, otherwise neither party would know what the facts are.

3. Explain that if the additional technical evidence is not forthcoming, then it will not be possible to test the evidence of the bank effectively or at all (this also implies that the bank will not be able to prove its case, because there will not be sufficient evidence put before the court).

4. Remind the judge that parties have a right to test the evidence under the first sentence of article 6 of the European Convention for the Protection of Human Rights and Fundamental Freedoms, which reads:

> 'In the determination of his civil rights and obligations or of any criminal charge against him, everyone is entitled to a fair and public hearing within a reasonable time by an independent and impartial tribunal established by law.'

Preparing the case

It is necessary that you to prepare properly for the trial, otherwise the lack of preparation will mean the case will probably not go well. When one or both parties are litigants in person, the judge will try to help, but the judge cannot take over the presentation of the case. This book is aimed at providing guidance to people who have a dispute with their bank. For this reason, it is anticipated that the claimant will probably be a litigant in person, and a solicitor and a barrister will represent the bank. If this is the case, then the bank will be well prepared. This means it is also necessary for you to be well prepared.

Preparation involves the following (this list is not exhaustive):

The expert

It will be necessary to find an expert (it is wise to find an expert very early on, and well before initiating legal action). It will be necessary to tell them about the dispute, and ask them for their advice. It is essential to find an expert that knows about banking systems. If the judge agrees that it is necessary to have expert evidence, they might order that both experts agree to meet to discuss what issues are in dispute. This is important, because such a meeting is not meant to allow the experts to agree on everything, but for them to set out what they agree about and what they do not agree about. The aim is to save time and money. For more information about expert witnesses and the form of the report they are required to submit to a court, see Practice Direction 35.

Witness statements

Each person giving evidence must provide a witness statement to the court before the trial. A witness statement must include be verified by a statement of truth, for which see Practice Direction 22.

The evidence and questions to ask the other party

Preparing the case properly is the most important aspect of taking legal action. Many deserving cases brought before civil courts do not succeed because a party has failed to prepare the evidence and arguments adequately. A thorough knowledge of the following is essential:

1. The technical details of the ATM system, point of sale system or internet banking system.

2. How ATMs, point of sale devices or internet banking can be subverted by thieves without the knowledge of the customer or the bank.

3. The weakness of electronic evidence and how to challenge the legal presumptions relating to electronic evidence.

4. The burden of proof (that is, which party has the duty of proving their case, and what they must do to prove their case).

It is necessary to have a file with all the relevant correspondence set out in date order. If the correspondence is only between you and the bank, then there is only need for one file. If the correspondence is between a number of other organisations, such as the police, Financial Ombudsman Service, and others, then it is better to file the correspondence in date order, but for each set of files to be in separate folders. An index for each set of correspondence is essential.

Create a list of points to make when presenting the case. This list should be in date order, and it should include references to the various letters or other evidence that will be included in the file.

Prepare a schedule of all the expenses associated with the claim, and have all the original receipts ready and filed.

If other witnesses are necessary to give evidence, other than the claimant and expert witness, it might be necessary to apply to the court for a witness summons. The court staff will offer advice on this matter.

The final hearing or trial

The judge will usually sit in open court to hear the case, unless there is a reason that it should be held in private.

The hearing is informal, and the strict rules of evidence do not apply in a small claims case. The judge can deal with the hearing as they see fit; they may ask questions of the witnesses, and they can restrict the amount of time a witness gives evidence.

At the end of the hearing, the judge may give judgment immediately. They must give their reasons for reaching their decision. If the matter is complex, the judge may decide to give judgment either orally at a later hearing or in writing.

Appeal

Either party has the right to appeal from the judgment of a judge, but only if the judge made a mistake in law, or there was a serious irregularity in the proceedings.

A notice of appeal must be filed within 21 days from the date of the decision.

Appendices

Appendix 1 98
Actions you should consider taking immediately where you have a problem with an ATM and PIN or a Point of Sale (PoS) purchase

Appendix 2 104
Excerpts from the Home Office Counting Rules for fraud and forgery

Appendix 3 105
Suggested text of a letter to send to the bank before taking legal action

Appendix 4 108
Sample Particulars of Claim for an internet banking claim

Appendix 5 112
Sample of a Particulars of Claim for an ATM or Point of Sale (PoS) claim

Appendix 6 116
Some questions to ask a solicitor before instructing them

Appendix 7 119
Some questions to ask of the bank if the bank has not provided the information at the disclosure stage of legal proceedings

Appendix 8 127
Guidance issued to customers on reducing ATM and online banking crime

Appendix 9 130
Fraud figures

Appendix 10 134
'Debit cards, ATMs and negligence of the bank and customer' [This article was first published in *Butterworths Journal of International Banking and Financial Law*, Volume 27, Number 3, March 2012, 163 – 173]

Appendix 11 163
'Electronic banking and how courts approach the evidence' [This article was published in the *Computer Law and Security Review*, Volume 29 Issue 2 (April 2013), 144 – 251]

Appendix 12 181
Further information

Appendix 1

Actions you should consider taking immediately where you have a problem with an ATM and PIN or a Point of Sale (PoS) purchase

The suggestions noted below are not legal advice, but suggestions that you might consider if you have difficulties in having any money refunded where money was removed from your account without your authority or knowledge. It must be emphasised, that the bank has to determine whether a customer is telling the truth when they say money was withdrawn without their authority or knowledge. Chips were introduced to cards to try to eliminate or reduce fraud, and the evidence that a chip was read can go some way to proving it was your card, and not a cloned card in the ATM, for instance.

It cannot be emphasised too much, that you need to act as a matter of urgency (that is, within 24 hours) if you find unauthorised withdrawals have been made from your account.

Before approaching your bank

Check receipts against your statements. It is easy to jump to the conclusion that you are not responsible for a withdrawal or payment because you do not remember the purpose of the payment. After some thought and cross checking of memories within the household (including looking at diaries), you might discover that all of the debits set out on your statement are correct.

If cash has been withdrawn from an ATM or ATMs, or goods or services bought using a card via a PoS in a shop, garage or restaurant, be honest with yourself and ask whether you have left your card around the home in a way that another member of the family, or a lodger, could have taken it without you knowing. This happens more frequently than some people like to admit.

Preserving evidence
Retain your card
> If you have your card in your possession, do not destroy it or give it to the bank. If an employee from the bank tells you to destroy the card, they are telling you to destroy evidence. A judge will not be impressed with such advice, because the information stored on the card is vital evidence that can help explain the cause of the dispute. Place the card in an envelope, seal the envelope, then

write your signature on the part of the envelope where the flap and the envelope meet, so if anybody opens or tampers with the envelope, it will be obvious. Keep the envelope somewhere safe.

You will need to have the transaction counter on your card checked by a digital evidence specialist. If the transaction counter on your card is less than the number of transactions recorded against your account, the evidence points to a cloned card being used by a thief to make withdrawals. It is wrong of the bank to tell you to destroy the card if it remains in your possession: this is the deliberate destruction of evidence, which is neither desirable nor appropriate.

Write a letter to your bank putting them on notice that they must retain all the records that are relevant to the dispute. Do not rely on conversations by telephone.

Ask your bank for copies of the ATM and PoS receipts.

Put your bank on notice that you wish to see the ARQC.
　The bank may refuse to permit you to see the ATM receipts and the ARQC, but if you put them on notice (send them a letter by recorded delivery) that you may rely upon these items of evidence to assess whether your card was used or not, and they then destroy the evidence before legal action takes place (if it does take place), then this will not be good for the bank.

Setting the expectations with the bank
If you have not engaged a solicitor, write a letter to the bank setting out that it will be required to prove that their records and systems are reliable and can be trusted.

Judges are likely to approach the reliability of computer systems much as they might once have approached the till roll from a mechanical cash register on the basis that it is reasonable to assume that the till roll correctly reflects the transactions entered on the till. Suitably qualified expert evidence will need to include explanations as to why it is not reasonable to make the corresponding assumption in the case of computer systems. This evidence needs to address the complexity and unpredictability of software in general, as well as making the point that when security is being assessed, it is necessary to consider the performance of the system when it is operating in the way it is designed to perform, but also when a highly motivated thief undermines its weaknesses. This evidence provides a strong foundation for arguing that the bank must prove all the links in the chain.

If the bank complains of the burden of proof because of the complexity of its systems, suitable expert evidence should be adduced about the need for systems to be simple enough to be easily checked if their reliability and security is to be maintained. This provides a foundation for alternative arguments, either that the tasks to be imposed on the bank are not unduly burdensome, or that the fact that those tasks are unduly burdensome is in itself evidence of the unreliability of those systems.

Obtaining evidence
Check the possibility that cctv footage might exist

Identify the physical location of the ATM, shop, garage or restaurant and photograph the ATM and relevant locations, including any signs of ccvt. It might be that cctv footage exists of those people using the ATM or ATMs in question. You will need to identify the owner of the relevant cctv, then request to have a copy of the footage from the owner. This might be far more difficult than it appears. Although the owners of cctv insist they are recording to prevent crime, many people have found obtaining cctv footage is almost impossible. In some cases, the police have told people that it is not their concern, and the police have informed the complainant that they must look to their bank to obtain such footage. Some banks will not cooperate with their customer over obtaining such footage, and often the bank or the police lose the cctv evidence.

There may also be technical problems with the actual cctv footage because of poor quality, and it might be that the footage is destroyed after a set period of time. If a policy exists to destroy all footage after 30 days, then any subject access request you might consider making under the provisions of the Data Protection Act 1998 will mean the footage is destroyed before the request is dealt with. Ideally, you should find out if any cctv footage is available, and obtain a copy immediately. If necessary, visit the shop or bank and ask to see the cctv manager, and get them to go through the recording and copy the recording for you. If you do this, you will be wise to ask them to give you a statement – if not, you should record the date and time you spoke to them, their name, address of the premises and any actions that were carried out. If the bank holds the cctv, put them on formal notice (send them a letter by recorded delivery) that you wish the evidence to be retained, pending any legal action.

Alibi

If you were at another location at the time the cash was withdrawn, recall who you were with and get them to make a statement for you immediately, preferably made before a solicitor. Evidence that you were somewhere else at the time the withdrawals were made will be very helpful. Do not delay in doing this. If you were on your own and shopping perhaps, retain evidence of any of the transactions you made, especially if they were with other cards in your possession.

Request your bank to provide a full copy of your customer file

You should have a contractual right to see your customer file, but if this is refused, make a subject access request under the provisions of the Data Protection Act 1998 (if you make an application under the provisions of the Act, you must follow the guidance issued by the Information Commissioner). This is important, because some thieves become employees of banks, with the deliberate intent of stealing from the bank and its customers. They convince the bank that they are ordinary people looking for work. They identify accounts and amend the postal address of the customer, make a request for a new card and cheque book, have them sent to the new address, and then their conspirators steal from the customer's account using the card and cheque book. The problem is, when the new card is used, the bank has evidence that a PIN was used, and will usually refuse to investigate the matter any further.

Practical tips

1. Consider approaching an experienced solicitor that is familiar with digital evidence for help.

2. Consider recording every conversation you have with your bank, and ensure the person you are speaking to is aware that you are recording the conversation. Obtain the name of the person you are speaking to, together with the name of their department and telephone number. Conversely, ask the person you are speaking to if the telephone conversation is being recorded. The bank usually records the conversation. You have the right to obtain a copy of the conversation.

3. Take full notes of every conversation if you cannot record the conversation. Ensure the person you are speaking to is aware that you are taking notes. Ensure the person you speak to is aware that you are the customer, and you should be treated with courtesy.

Some employees are very aggressive towards customers claiming money has been debited from their account for which they are not responsible, and it is important to remind the employee that you are the customer.

4. Where your card is used to buy good or services from a shop or online seller of goods or services, and your bank refuses to accept that you were not responsible for the transaction, write or go to the shop or provider to ask for a copy of the transaction slip. One person the author is aware of did this, and the shop owner sent them a copy of the transaction slip, which proved to their bank that the transaction had not been undertaken by chip and PIN, even though the bank insisted that the transaction had been carried out by chip and PIN. In this case, the bank insisted that the customer was responsible for buying goods in Turkey, yet the customer had never visited the country, and the bank only paid the money back to the customer when the customer presented the bank with evidence to prove their computer systems were at fault.

Other people might have the same problem as you

Do not delay in trying to find out if other people had the same problem with the same ATM. This is also very helpful, and you must do this quickly – ask your local newspaper if they will run a story, start a web site to ask for help, put up posters for the names and address of anybody else that might have had an identical experience.

Report the matter to the police

The police will probably not be interested in taking up your complaint. There are two reasons for this. First, in general, the police do not investigate one in three crimes reported to them, as reported by *The Times* newspaper (Saturday 30 July 2011, pages 1 and 10). Crimes relating to ATMs and online banking are expensive to investigate and require those officers conducting the investigation to have sufficient knowledge to conduct an investigation competently. Few police officers have the necessary qualifications or expertise.

Second, the official position is that it is for the bank to make a complaint to the police that a crime has been committed, because the bank is the one that has lost money. This would be correct if the bank refunds your money. However, where the bank refuses to refund your money, then they are, in effect, accusing you of fraud by asking for the return of money you say that you neither withdrew yourself, nor authorised any other person to withdraw.

In this respect, it will be worth considering submitting a request for information under the Freedom of Information Act 2000 to the local police to find out if other people living locally and using the same ATM have had the same problem as you.

You might request information such as:

i. The number of crime reports (set out on a monthly basis over the material time withdrawals were made – perhaps three months either side) recorded in the relevant town, city or village relating to complaints made by individuals.

ii. Where withdrawals have been recorded

iii Where the individual claimed they were not responsible for the withdrawal.

Consider writing to your MP

Write to your Member of Parliament. This is suggested for two reasons. First, if every MP received regular letters of complaint from their constituents on this topic, then they would exert pressure on government ministers to do something about the present system of recording and handling unauthorised withdrawals from ATMs.

Second, sometimes the only way you can obtain help is by going to your MP. Sometimes an MP can resolve the issue with a single letter to the Chairman of the bank. Some MPs will react to you by not doing anything, with the lame excuse that your case might go before the courts. In the vast majority of cases, this is impractical for the person that has suffered a loss, because they cannot afford legal help, and do not want to be faced with the uncertainty of paying the costs of the bank if they do not succeed. The risks of taking legal action can be very high for a variety of reasons.

Consider approaching the media

If all else fails, you might consider telling members of the press and media of your dispute. This sometimes has the effect of publicising your case, with the result that and you can benefit with a quick and satisfactory conclusion. This has been effective for a number of people in the past. However, it is wise to give very careful consideration to this option, because you cannot be certain how your case will be dealt with, and you might have to face the possibility of adverse comments that could be very hurtful.

Appendix 2

Excerpts from the Home Office Counting Rules for fraud and forgery

Available at:
https://www.gov.uk/government/uploads/system/uploads/attachment_data/file/177109/count-fraud-april-2013.pdf

53C Fraud by False Representation Cheque, Plastic Card and Online Bank Accounts (not PSP)

RECORDING PRACTICE: CHEQUE AND PLASTIC CARD FRAUD

Action Fraud will not record the original theft of items used to commit this fraud. Customers of the Financial Institutions will be asked to report the theft of items separately to Police where appropriate. In these instances Police should record the original theft of the card etc under the appropriate class. It is not necessary to record another crime if the theft is already recorded or included in another principle crime e.g. burglary or robbery.

RECORDING PRACTICE: CONSPIRACY TO DEFRAUD

If, following receipt of information, there is evidence that suggests that plastic cards are being compromised at a particular location on a regular basis, and no crimes have been confirmed for this location with individual financial institutions, this should be recorded as one offence of Conspiracy to Defraud (class NFIB5A), by the Police. Details should also be passed to the NFIB.

Appendix 3

Suggested text of a letter to send to the bank before taking legal action

Note: this letter has been prepared for unauthorised withdrawals at ATMs, so it will need a slight adjustment if you have problems with online banking. An earlier version of this letter was written by the author and added to the Which? web site as a free download in November 2011, with the express permission of the author.

[INSERT THE DATE]

[INSERT YOUR HOME ADDRESS]

[INSERT THE NAME OF YOUR BANK]

[INSERT THE ADDRESS OF BANK]

Dear Sir or Madam,

[Provide a reference: perhaps your card number or account number, or both]

I write to confirm that there [is a transaction] [are a number of transactions] that have occurred on my account that I did not make or authorise. The transaction(s) I dispute are:

[DATE] [DESCRIPTION] [AMOUNT]
(put each transaction on a separate line if more than one)

Because I did not authorise the transaction(s) I have listed above, regulation 61 of the Payment Services Regulations 2009 requires you to refund the amount in dispute immediately, and to restore my account to the state it would have been in had the unauthorised payment transaction(s) not taken place.

Regulation 60 of the Payment Services Regulations requires you to prove that the payment transaction was authenticated, accurately recorded, entered in your accounts, and not affected by a technical breakdown or some other deficiency. For this reason, if I have to take any further action, you have to provide sufficient evidence of each of these points.

I put you on notice that you have a duty to preserve all the items of relevant evidence both in support of and against the dispute. I will retain a copy of this letter to show a judge, should you put me in the position of taking legal action to recover the money, and if you fail to provide the evidence.

[If you still have your card] I have retained my [debit card] [credit card], and I will keep it so that it can be tested by an independent digital evidence specialist. This is important, because the card includes an Application Transaction Counter (ATC). The ATC is increased by one each time a transaction takes place. A test of the card will help to determine whether the ATC has been increased, and the test can enable a comparison of the transactions recorded on my statements to establish whether there are any discrepancies.

[If the card issuer has asked (or told) you to destroy the card, it will be necessary to consider including the following text, or something similar] You have requested me to destroy the card(s) you have issued to me. If I undertook this action, I would be destroying evidence. You are aware that the card contains valuable evidence in the Application Transaction Counter. For this reason it is improper of you to require me to destroy evidence.

[If the card issuer told you to destroy the card, and you followed the instructions of the bank, it will be necessary to consider including the following text, or something similar] You informed me to destroy my card [it will be helpful to give the name of the person who told you to do this, together with the date and time, if this was over the telephone; if the instructions were written in a letter, you should refer to the letter]. I have destroyed the card in accordance with your instructions. However, I have now become aware that the card includes an Application Transaction Counter (ATC). The ATC is increased by one each time a transaction takes place. A test of the card would have helped to determine whether the ATC had been increased, and the test could have enabled a comparison of the transactions recorded on my statements to establish whether there are any discrepancies. As a direct result of you telling me to destroy my card, you have deliberately requested me to destroy evidence, knowing that legal proceedings may be taken by me to recover the money. If I have cause to take legal action, I will bring this matter to the attention of the judge, and you will be required to explain to the judge why you instructed me to destroy relevant evidence.

You are welcome to contact me on [INSERT YOUR TELEPHONE NUMBER] to discuss the matter.

Yours faithfully,

[SIGN YOUR NAME]

[TYPE YOUR NAME]

Appendix 4

Sample Particulars of Claim for an internet banking claim

Initial remarks

On the reverse of the claim form (N1), there is a box headed 'Particulars of Claim'. There might be sufficient space to write all of the details on the form. If there is not enough space, then the Particulars of Claim can be produced on a separate sheet (or sheets) of paper and handed in with the form. If a separate sheet of paper is used, it is necessary to provide all of the information included in the sample Particulars of Claim.

The purpose of a Particulars of Claim is set out in Practice Direction 16 Rule 16.4. It must include a concise statement of the facts on which you rely, and if you claim interest, you must explicitly claim it, and the basis on which it is claimed. A Particulars of Claim does not include any evidence. (For more information, see David Emmett, *Drafting* (Oxford University Press) – this useful text is published every year, so if you decide to obtain a copy, you need to find the most recent edition).

Notes on the Particulars of Claim

Name of County Court: insert the name of the court in which the claim will be submitted

Claim number: leave blank (the court will allocate the claim with a number after the claim has been submitted)

Your name:
   (a) If you are making a claim in your own name, you must include your name in full, e.g. Samantha Georgina Roberstonia

   (b) If you are making a claim because the account is your business, then you need to provide the following:

   If it is a limited company, the full name of the limited company should appear, e.g. 'The Plastic Company Limited'

If the company is not limited, you must put the name of the company and your name, e.g. 'Samantha Georgina Roberstonia trading as The Plastic Company'

Name of the defendant: It is important to get the name of the defendant correct, otherwise your claim might be rejected. Look carefully at any agreement you have signed with your bank, because the correct name of the bank will be given in the agreement. For instance, if you have an account with Halifax, the correct name would be 'BANK OF SCOTLAND PLC (trading as HALIFAX)'.

Paragraph 1: It is necessary to indicate that you have an account with the bank. That is the purpose of the first paragraph. It is necessary to include the branch of the bank that you bank with. In the case of an internet-only bank, then it will probably be the head office.

Paragraph 2: It is necessary to set out the loss you have incurred.

Paragraph 3: This paragraph indicates that you are not responsible for the withdrawals set out in paragraph 2.

Paragraph 4: This paragraph sets out the contractual basis for your claim, and provides the legal basis for the claim, also called the 'cause of action'.

Paragraph 5: This paragraph makes it clear the amount that is in dispute.

Paragraph 6: This paragraph sets out the claim for interest (for more details, see Practice Direction 16 Rule 16.4.). The rate of interest depends on the type of claim that you are making. For more information, speak to the court.

The summary of the claim (the text that follows on from paragraph 6): the summary should include:

(a) What you want the court to decide.

(b) Your claim for the debits that are the subject of the claim.

(c) If you are permitted to claim legal costs, a claim for legal costs (you cannot claim for legal costs in small claims procedures).

(d) If you are permitted to claim the cost of a lawyer, a claim for solicitor's costs (you cannot claim for solicitor's costs in small claims procedures).

(e) The claim for interest.

IN THE [ ] COUNTY COURT   CLAIM NO. [ ]

BETWEEN:

                Your name or name of company

                                                                Claimant

                              and

                                  [ ]

                                                                   Defendant

                          PARTICULARS OF CLAIM

1. The Defendant is a bank carrying on business at its branch at [ ] and elsewhere. The Claimant has an account at this branch ("the Account").

2. On [day] [month] [year], the Defendant debited the sums of money set out below from the Claimant's account by honouring instructions purporting to be initiated by way of the internet by the use of a username and password and other information determined by the Defendant (those acts together constituting an "electronic signature"), purportedly by the Claimant on the Account. The Defendant debited the Account.

                                         Particulars

[day] [month] [year] [reference as given in your statement] £ [ ]

[day] [month] [year] [reference as given in your statement] £ [ ]

                                                                            Total £ [ ]

3. The Claimant neither obtained access to the internet, nor entered the username and password or any other information determined by the Defendant for each of the transactions, nor made any electronic signature thereby constituted, and the Claimant's electronic signature used was a forgery.

4. Accordingly, the Defendant had no authority to debit the Account with the Claimant's Account with the amount of £ [ ]. The cause of action upon which the Claimant will rely is on the breach of contract by the Defendants for indebiting the account without authority.

5. For these reasons, the Clamant is entitled to and claims repayment of the sum of £ [ ].

6. Further the Claimant is entitled to and claims interest pursuant to section 69 of the County Courts Act 1984 on the sum of £ [ ] at the rate of [ ] per cent a year from [day] [month] [year], amounting to £ [ ] at [day] [month] [year] and continuing at a daily rate of £ [ ].

AND the Claimant claims:
1) A declaration that the Defendant was not entitled to debit the Account with the amounts withdrawn.
2) £ [ ].
3) Legal costs. [If relevant]
4) Solicitor's costs. [If relevant]
5) The claimant claims interest under section 69 of the County Courts Act 1984 at the rate of [ ] per cent a year from [date when the money became owed to you] to [date you are issuing the claim] of £[amount] and also interest at the same rate up to the date of judgment or earlier payment at a daily rate of [daily rate of interest].

Dated this [day] [month] [year]

The Claimant believes that the facts stated in this Particulars of Claim are true.

Appendix 5

Sample Particulars of Claim for an ATM or Point of Sale (PoS) claim

Initial remarks

On the reverse of the claim form (N1), there is a box headed 'Particulars of Claim'. There might be sufficient space to write all of the details on the form. If there is not enough space, then the Particulars of Claim can be produced on a separate sheet (or sheets) of paper and handed in with the form. If a separate sheet of paper is used, it is necessary to provide all of the information included in the sample Particulars of Claim.

The purpose of a Particulars of Claim is set out in Practice Direction 16 Rule 16.4. It must include a concise statement of the facts on which you rely, and if you claim interest, you must explicitly claim it, and the basis on which it is claimed. A Particulars of Claim does not include any evidence. (For more information, see David Emmett, *Drafting* (Oxford University Press) – this useful text is published every year, so if you decide to obtain a copy, you need to find the most recent edition).

Notes on the Particulars of Claim

Name of County Court: insert the name of the court in which the claim will be submitted

Claim number: leave blank (the court will allocate the claim with a number after the claim has been submitted)

Your name:
　(a) If you are making a claim in your own name, you must include your name in full, e.g. Samantha Georgina Roberstonia

　(b) If you are making a claim because the account is your business, then you need to provide the following:

　　If a limited company, the full name of the limited company, e.g. 'The Plastic Company Limited'

　　If the company is not limited, you must put the name of the company and your name, e.g. 'Samantha Georgina

Roberstonia trading as The Plastic Company'

Name of the defendant: It is important to get the name of the defendant correct, otherwise your claim might be rejected. Look carefully at any agreement you have signed with your bank, because the correct name of the bank will be given in the agreement. For instance, if you have an account with Halifax, the correct name would be 'BANK OF SCOTLAND PLC (trading as HALIFAX)'.

Paragraph 1: It is necessary to indicate that you have an account with the bank. That is the purpose of the first paragraph. It is necessary to include the branch of the bank that you bank with. In the case of an internet-only bank, then it will be the head office.

Paragraph 2: It is necessary to set out the loss you have incurred.

Paragraph 3: This paragraph indicates that you are not responsible for the withdrawals set out in paragraph 2.

Paragraph 4: This paragraph sets out the contractual basis for your claim, and provides the legal basis for the claim, also called the 'cause of action'.

Paragraph 5: This paragraph makes it clear the amount that is in dispute.

Paragraph 6: This paragraph sets out the claim for interest (for more details, see Practice Direction 16 Rule 16.4.). The rate of interest depends on the type of claim that you are making. For more information, speak to the court.

The summary of the claim (the text that follows on from paragraph 6): the summary should include:

(a) What you want the court to decide.

(b) Your claim for the debits that are the subject of the claim.

(c) If you are permitted to claim legal costs, a claim for legal costs (you cannot claim for legal costs in small claims procedures).

(d) If you are permitted to claim the cost of a lawyer, a claim for solicitor's costs (you cannot claim for solicitor's costs in small claims procedures).

(e) The claim for interest.

IN THE [   ] COUNTY COURT   CLAIM NO. [   ]

BETWEEN:

                Your name or name of company

                                                                                      Claimant

                and

                [ ]

                                                                                Defendant

                PARTICULARS OF CLAIM

1. The Defendant is a bank carrying on business at its branch at [ ] and elsewhere. The Claimant has an account at this branch ("the Account").

2. On the dates and at the times listed in the table below, the Defendant paid sums of money in cash through automated teller machines ("ATM") on the Account payable in cash [and/or through Point of Sale terminals ("POS")] in respect of payment for services and goods. The Defendant debited the Account with the amounts of each ATM transaction [and/or POS transaction].

Date	Time [if known]	Amount	ATM (physical location) or POS (and physical location if known)	ATM Number [if known]

3 The Claimant neither used the card issued to him or her by the Defendants for each or any of the transactions, nor entered his or her personal identification number, nor made any electronic signature thereby constituted, and did not authorise or enable the card to be used for the withdrawals in the ATMs [and/or POS terminals], and the Claimant's electronic signature used in the ATMs [and/or POS terminals] was a forgery.

4 Accordingly, the Defendant had no authority to dispense the cash from the ATMs [or authorise the debit of sums in respect of the goods and services by way of the POS terminals] and was not entitled to debit the Account with the amounts withdrawn from the ATMs [and/or POS terminals]. The cause of action upon which the Claimant will rely is on the breach of contract by the Defendants for indebiting the Claimant's account without authority.

5 For these reasons, the Clamant is entitled to and claims repayment of the sum of £ [ ].

6 Further the Claimant is entitled to and claims interest pursuant to section 69 of the County Courts Act 1984 on the sum of £ [ ] at the rate of [ ] per cent a year from [day] [month] [year], amounting to £ [ ] at [day] [month] [year] and continuing at a daily rate of £ [ ].

AND the Claimant claims:
1) A declaration that the Defendant was not entitled to debit the Account with the amounts withdrawn from the ATMs.
2) £ [ ].
3) Legal costs. [If relevant]
4) Solicitor's costs. [If relevant]
5) The claimant claims interest under section 69 of the County Courts Act 1984 at the rate of [ ] per cent a year from [date when the money became owed to you] to [date you are issuing the claim] of £[amount] and also interest at the same rate up to the date of judgment or earlier payment at a daily rate of [daily rate of interest].

Dated this [day] [month] [year]

The Claimant believes that the facts stated in this Particulars of Claim are true.

Appendix 6

Some questions to ask a solicitor before instructing them

Questions to ask a solicitor about their fees

1. What is their hourly rate? Do they consider a fixed fee?

2. How do they charge their hourly rate – that is, by the full hour, or a proportion of an hour [at 6 minute intervals]?

3. What do they charge for? Ask them for a detailed breakdown of all the fees that they will apply. This is important, because some firms of solicitors include additional charges into their terms of work, which are not easy to notice unless you read every page of the Client Care Letter sent to the client when the client agrees to be represented by the solicitor.

4. Will they do the work or will a junior solicitor do the work? If a junior solicitor will do the work, what is their hourly rate and their experience in such matters?

5. When writing letters on your behalf, will they copy all of the information you have given them and put it in to any letter they send on your behalf? (That is, information from the papers and copies of letters you have given them). If they copy this information into any letter they write, they will charge you more.

Questions to ask about their knowledge of banking, ATMs and internet accounts

Digital evidence

1. What do they know about digital evidence?

2. Do they know that computer systems are not reliable? [Find out if they have read Chapter 5 of Stephen Mason, general editor, *Electronic Evidence* (3rd edn, LexisNexis Butterworths, 2012)]

3. Do they know the tests for authenticating electronic evidence? [Find out if they have read Chapter 4 of Stephen Mason, general editor, *Electronic Evidence* (3rd edn, LexisNexis Butterworths, 2012)]

4. What case law is there in relation to electronic evidence and banking disputes? [There is, see Stephen Mason, 'Debit cards, ATMs and negligence of the bank and customer', *Butterworths Journal of International Banking and Financial Law*, Volume 27, Number 3, March 2012, 163 – 173; Stephen Mason, 'Electronic banking and how courts approach the evidence', *Computer Law and Security Review*, Volume 29, Issue 2 (April 2013), 144 – 151; also see also various issues of the *Digital Evidence and Electronic Signature Law Review*.]

Electronic signatures

1. What do they know about electronic signatures? (If you use an e-mail, PIN, send text messages, buy anything online, you use an electronic signature).

2. What case law is there in relation to electronic signatures? [There is, for which see Stephen Mason, *Electronic Signatures in Law* (3rd edn, Cambridge University Press, 2012)]

3. Ask them what 'non-repudiation' means. [It is not a legal term, and is meaningless in law, but unless the lawyer knows who uses it and why they use it, they will not understand this term and might then agree something with the other side that they should not. There is an in-depth analysis of this term in Stephen Mason, *Electronic Signatures in Law*.]

Banking

1. Ask them what the burden of proof is in your case: in other words, which party has to prove what.

2. Ask them to outline the banking system from the moment you put your card in to an ATM to the moment a payment is debited from your account (as you can imagine, this is quite complex, and there are a number of third parties involved in the chain that the bank will enter sub-contracts with).

3. Ask them how they will gather evidence of previous attacks on ATMs.

4. Ask them the various mechanisms by which a thief can use a forged card or obtain your PIN after you have had your card stolen.

Their experience

1. Ask them how many ATM or internet banking disputes they have dealt with.

2. If they have represented a client in an ATM or internet banking dispute, ask them who the most knowledgeable experts are to ask to offer expert advice.

3. Ask them if they will conduct the entire case themselves, including the hearing in the court.

4. If they will not appear for you in court, ask them for the name (chambers and web site) of the barrister they will brief to represent you in court.

5. Ask the solicitor to tell you what experience the barrister has with digital evidence and electronic signatures.

Appendix 7

Some questions to ask of the bank if the bank has not provided the information at the disclosure stage of legal proceedings

In the event of a dispute, it may be necessary to ask your bank a range of questions about the ATM or ATMs in question, where a transactions takes place without the card (called 'card not present'), and where a transaction is in a shop, garage or restaurant at a 'point of sale'. The bank should give you this information at the correct time in the legal proceedings, should you decide to begin legal action. It might be helpful to ask these questions of your bank immediately you have discovered unauthorised withdrawals, because many banks delete records regularly.

If the bank will not give you the information, you will have to consider asking a judge to order the bank to give you the information. The bank might claim that much of the information listed below is commercially confidential, and that you are on what is called a 'fishing expedition' and asking for information that is not relevant, so you will need to ensure that you have good arguments for making the request. For this reason, it is important to concentrate on only asking for information that is directly relevant to the dispute.

For obvious reasons, if you consider taking legal action, it is crucial to get an IT banking specialist to advise you, and to consider acting as your expert witness. The list below is only a guide, and is not a substitute for the advice of a person with specialist knowledge in this area.

Some of the issues to cover include:

The card

Which card was alleged to have been used (if the bank cannot identify this, they cannot justify their assertion that your card was used). Sometimes a bank might issue several cards with the same card number on the front (one for the wife, one for the husband), but the principal account number sequence number should be different, which is sometimes printed on the card.

The transaction

The time(s) and dates(s) of the transaction(s)

A full copy of the charge slip (paper if physical, otherwise electronic)

Charge-back records for the acquired merchant (it is important to know if the merchant has a high fraud rate)

If a transaction takes place where the card with a chip is physically present:

What the Application Transaction Counter (ATC) was

Whether there were any transaction attempts recorded with duplicate ATCs

What, where and when were the transactions with immediately prior and post ATCs.

Whether the transaction was recorded as 'PIN verified'

If the transaction is related to the card not being present:

The IP address from which the transaction was conducted

Details of the PCI Security Standards Council Data Security Standards (PCI-DSS) compliance of the acquired merchant including the last Qualified Security Assessors (QSA) report

Full details of the shipment and billing addresses provided for the transaction

Details of any 'Verified by Visa' or 'MasterCard Securecode' interaction (such as IP address, the password used, full or partial password)

Any reset of 'Verified by Visa' or 'MasterCard Securecode' passwords in the month before the disputed transactions

The location of the transaction

Whether the ATM was owned and managed by the bank, or owned by the bank and managed by a third party, or owned and managed by a third party

Whether that ATM had a security module (cryptographic processor) as part of the machine

Whether its terminal could be offline

What actions would cause the ATM to accept fallback

What the ATM's fallback policy was and how it is enforced

Whether the ATM accepted fallback

Who the acquiring bank was (that is, the bank or financial institution that accepted the transaction)

Whether they retained authentication logs, and for long; how long they are required to retain the logs (and the authority for retention and disposal); what the industry standard is for retaining logs

Whether your bank informed all the parties in the chain of the possibility of the dispute

Further relevant information, including knowledge about third party links, such as:

Where the message was sent

The agents through which the message was sent

Whether they had a security module (cryptographic processor), and if they did, that make of security module was used, and the version of the software

How many links there were in the chain to the issuing bank – each of these might need to be identified

Who retained the authentication logs

The period of time it is necessary to retain the logs

The date and time were they notified of the dispute

The bank

The identity of the issuing bank

Whether any of the processing is outsourced to a third party, and if so, identify the organisation to which it is outsourced

Whether they have a security module (cryptographic processor, including the make of security module and the version of software)

What measures, if any, were taken to prevent a corrupt employee from finding out the PIN by taking advantage of a design flaw in the hardware security module (HSM) used to protect the PIN (this is called an API attack because this form of attack exploits a weakness in the Application Programming Interface of the HSM)

Whether they retained the authentication logs, and how long for

The period of time they are required to retain the logs

The industry standard for retaining logs

The date and time were they notified of the dispute

What data items were recorded on the various (up to three) tracks of the magnetic strip of the card in dispute (i.e. CVV, specific card identifier details, that is whether there are more details other than the PAN)

Information that might be relevant include the security modules (cryptographic processor) (an item of hardware that it resistant to being tampered with)

The operations performed by the security module

The make of security module

The version of the software

What measures, if any, were taken to prevent a corrupt employee from finding out the PIN by taking advantage of a design flaw in the hardware security module (HSM) used to protect the PIN (called an API attack because this form of attack exploits a weakness in the Application Programming Interface of the HSM)

Whether the relevant ATMs were chip-enabled at the time of the transactions

Whether the relevant ATMs were fitted with a chip and pin reader

At what date these were brought into service for reading chip cards

On what date, if any, ATMs were programmed to not accept magnetic-strip transactions from any card that should have had a chip

Verification of the PIN

Whether offline PIN verification takes place at the discretion of any party or whether it is mandatory that the PIN is encrypted at the ATM and sent to the issuer for verification

How this policy is enforced (this is relevant because it tends to indicate that the PIN was verified by the issuer)

Whether some ATMs allow local verification on the card

If an ATM is off-line, whether it checks the PIN

Evidence

Evidence that the bank should be expected to provide in evidence includes the following:

1. EMV logs of the ARQC, ARPC and TC as recorded at the acquiring bank, the issuing bank and the switch (and any third party in the chain).

Whether the PIN verified before the ARQC was generated.

(a) To find this out it is necessary to know the detailed format used by the bank to generate the Authorisation Request Cryptogram (ARQC), which may contain information signifying whether the PIN was verified. Among other things it is necessary to have the Application Transaction Counter (ATC) and the Issuer Application Data (IAD) – one of the IAD fields should specify whether the PIN was verified.

(b) If the information has been destroyed, the reason must be given because (i) the EMV protocol says this data is evidence of the transaction and (ii) the evidence will have been destroyed in the knowledge that legal proceedings might take place (this is because the bank will have been alerted to the dispute very quickly, and should have issued orders for the relevant evidence to be retained in the event it is necessary to prove the case in legal proceedings).

2. If the bank claims their program and print-out proves the transaction took place, it is necessary for the bank to prove their program is reliable and trustworthy.

3. Where there is reliance on bespoke software instead of the logs, it is necessary to understand the software in order to test its reliability and trustworthiness in court, which means the bank should be requested to supply the full documentation, including any testing documentation (that is, whether the software worked and if was not tested, how the bank can say that it does or does not work).

4. Whether there was a reliance on VISA accreditation; if there is reliance on accreditation, what 'evaluation' means, and whether it is Common Criteria Evaluated or Common Criteria Certified. It is necessary to establish the difference between Common Criteria Evaluated and Common Criteria Certified, and if the bank is using Common Criteria, the question is why it is not certified (it might have been withdrawn from evaluation without failing, because a new version has been released); in addition, it is necessary to know who carried out the Evaluation or Certification, the criteria it was based on, who conducted the evaluation, and it will be helpful to request a copy of the evaluation and audit reports.

5. Evaluation and audit reports are important documents that can reveal weaknesses in the internal banking systems that the bank will prefer you not to know about. A bank will resist most strongly any claim that they should not have to reveal the findings of such reports. They will argue that such reports are highly sensitive and confidential, and that for this reason, the judge should not order the disclosure of such reports. However, a judge can order the disclosure of such a report with a duty imposed by the court on the recipient to treat the report in confidence. Should the recipient then breach the confidence imposed by the judge, the person in breach will be liable for contempt of court.

Two Examples

John Rusnak gambled on the differences in trading between the US dollar and the Yen in 1996, when Allfirst Financial Inc., and Allfirst Bank employed him. His total losses amounted to US$691 million. In the same was as Nick Leeson, John Rusnak used the failure of the bank to control the internal system to conceal his losses. He was duly charged, entered a plea of guilty, and sentenced to seven and a half years in prison and ordered to pay US$1,000 a month for five years after his release.

Kim David Faithfull was the bank manager at the Bennett Street branch of the Commonwealth Bank in Karratha, Australia. After the members of staff went home, he stole from term deposit accounts and foreign currency notes by transferring money directly into an online betting account with International All SportsBet. In all, he stole and lost A$18,998,309 over a period of five years. The bank did not know he was stealing from the bank until he gave himself up. He was sentenced to five years imprisonment.

In both of these examples, and many other similar examples, when the audit took place (whether an internal audit or an external audit), one of two results occurred:

1. Initially, the auditors failed to discover the thefts or method used to manipulate the computer systems.

2. When an auditor noticed how the system could be manipulated,

no action was taken to rectify the problem, or where action was undertaken, it was carried out much later.

The observations regarding evaluation and audit reports illustrate two important points:

1. The quality, knowledge and experience of the person conducting the audit are important. If the person conducting the audit does not have the necessary qualifications and experience, they will not know where to look for problems, and will not uncover discrepancies.

2. Where a person is nominated to conduct an audit without the necessary qualifications and experience, questions have to be asked as to why the auditor was appointed instead of an appropriately qualified and experienced person.

The fact is, evaluation and audit reports are an important aspect of modern banking, and therefore should be considered as evidence in a banking case.

Appendix 8

Guidance issued to customers on reducing ATM and online banking crime

Advice for telephone and online banking users is provided by Financial Fraud Action UK on their web site at http://www.financialfraudaction.org.uk/

In 2008, APACS wrote a short paper entitled *Personal Security Plan The best ways to minimise your chances of becoming a victim of fraud* (APACS, 2008). Although APACS has been closed, the tips are still available at http://www.ukpayments.org.uk/files/publications/exisiting_publications/general/apacspersonalsecurityplan2008.pdf

European Union – golden rules to reduce ATM crime

The guidance set out below is taken, with permission, from *ATM crime: Overview of the European situation and golden rules on how to avoid it* (European Network and Information Security Agency, August 2009), pages 24 and 25 http://www.enisa.europa.eu/activities/cert/security-month/deliverables/2009/atmcrime-de

These safety tips draw on analysis of data and available research. This section [of the paper] is intended to provide, in one convenient place, recommendations to raise awareness about the various types of crimes being carried out, with advice on how to spot them.

These rules offer maximum protection for the least amount of effort. By following these rules interested parties will increase their protection when they using an ATM.

Category		*Recommendations*	*Description*
Choose a safe ATM machine	1	Don't use ATMs with excessive signage or warnings	Don't use ATMs with excessive signage or warnings posted on the machine as they are often used by fraudsters to try and assure the public that ATMs that have been tampered with are safe. Be especially cautious of unusual instructions on how to operate the ATM.

Category		Recommendations	Description
	2	Use ATMs inside banks	When possible use ATMs inside banks, other buildings and enclosed areas, rather than on the street. ATMs on the street are easier for criminals to access.
	3	Don't use free standing ATMs	Avoid free standing ATMs that are in the open. Avoid ATMs that are not bolted to the side of a building or secured inside a facility. If the machine offers no fees but it is attached to a building and everything processes properly, you are probably fine.
Observe your physical surroundings	4	Be aware of the surroundings	Always be aware of your physical surroundings. Use an ATM which is in clear view and well lit. Be extra careful of machines in dark areas or in places that don't look well guarded and monitored.
	5	Check that people in the queue are at reasonable distance	Check that other people in the queue are a reasonable distance away from you. Be cautious if strangers offer to help you at an ATM, even if your card is stuck or you're having difficulties. Do not allow anyone to distract you.
	6	Protect your PIN by standing close to the ATM and shielding the key pad	Shield the keypad with your hand as you enter your PIN to prevent a hidden camera or a person from capturing your information. Never reveal your PIN to anyone.
Observe the ATM	7	Pay attention to the front of machines	If the front of the machine looks different from others in the area (for example, it has an extra mirror on the face), has sticky residue on it (potentially from a device attached to it) or extra signage, use a different machine and notify bank management with your concerns.

Category		Recommendations	Description
	8	Pay close attention to the slot you slide in your card	If you're visiting an unfamiliar ATM machine that is not inside a bank, examine it carefully for devices. Even if you are familiar with an ATM machine, pay attention to any differences or unusual characteristics of the card reader. If the slot looks strange or bulky, try to push on it with your hand. If something has been stuck over the real reader it will wiggle or even come off. Card or cash trapping devices need to be glued or taped to the card reader or cash dispenser. If the ATM appears to have anything stuck onto the card slot or keypad, do not use it. Cancel the transaction and walk away. Never try to remove suspicious devices.
	9	Pay close attention to the ATM's PIN pad	Even if you are familiar with an ATM machine, pay attention to any differences or unusual characteristics of the ATM's PIN pad. If a fake PIN pad has been stuck over the real pad it will appear "incorrectly attached" when being moved a bit back and forth.
	10	See if there are extra cameras	Look for 'extra' cameras beyond the basic and generally obvious ATM security camera.
	11	Report confiscated cards immediately	Report confiscated cards immediately. If you can, don't leave the machine. Instead call the bank from the ATM where your card was taken. Never rely on the help of strangers to retrieve a confiscated card. In addition notify your local law enforcement.

Appendix 8

Appendix 9

Fraud Figures

The figures for fraud in relation to financial transactions produced by Financial Fraud Action UK (previously APACS) indicate, in general terms, that certain types of fraud have been reduced since the introduction of digital signatures on the chip of a card, in association with an electronic signature in the form of a personal identity number (PIN). In this respect, the card issuers have had some success in reducing the risks associated with the use of technology that customers are required to use.

However, the fraud figures do not tell the whole story. This appendix considers the fraud figures produced by Financial Fraud Action UK, and suggests that some data is missing. Without the complete data, it is not possible to know how many people are affected by fraud in the UK every year, nor exactly how much fraud there is actually taking place.

It is useful to begin with the fraud figures produced by Financial Fraud Action UK, set out in tables 1 and 2.

Table 1

Annual fraud losses on cards issued in the UK 1995 – 2004 (all figures in £millions) (the figures have been rounded, which means the sum of separate items might differ from the totals)

Year / Type of fraud	1995	1996	1997	1998	1999	2000	2001	2002	2003	2004
Card not present	4.5	6.5	10.0	13.6	29.3	72.9	95.7	110.1	122.1	150.8
Counterfeit	7.7	13.3	20.3	26.8	50.3	107.1	160.4	148.5	110.6	129.7
Lost or stolen	60.1	60.0	66.2	65.8	79.7	101.9	114.0	108.3	112.4	114.4
Not received	9.1	10.0	12.5	12.0	14.6	17.7	26.8	37.1	45.1	72.9
'Identity theft'	1.8	7.2	13.1	16.8	14.4	17.4	14.6	20.6	30.2	36.9

Year / Type of fraud	1995	1996	1997	1998	1999	2000	2001	2002	2003	2004
UK Total	62.1	71.6	92.8	100.1	134.1	213.4	273.0	294.4	316.3	412.3
ATM fraud	3.5	4.4	8.2	9.7	12.2	18.3	21.2	29.1	41.1	74.6
Online banking fraud										12.2

Table 2

Annual fraud losses on cards issued in the UK 2005 – 2012 (all figures in £millions) (the figures have been rounded, which means the sum of separate items might differ from the totals)

Year / Type of fraud	2005	2006	2007	2008	2009	2010	2011	2012
Card not present	183.2	212.6	290.5	328.4	266.4	226.9	220.9	245.8
Counterfeit	96.8	99.6	144.3	169.8	80.9	47.6	36.1	42.1
Lost or stolen	89.0	68.4	56.2	54.1	47.9	44.4	50.1	55.2
Not received	40.0	15.4	34.1	47.4	38.2	38.1	11.3	12.8
'Identity theft'	30.5	31.9	10.2	10.2	6.9	8.4	22.5	32.1
UK Total	439.4	428.0	535.2	609.9	440.3	365.4	341.0	388.0
ATM fraud	65.8	61.9	35.0	45.7	36.7	33.2	29.3	28.9
Online banking fraud	23.2	33.5	22.6	52.5	59.7	46.7	35.4	39.6

Appendix 9

Notes:

1. 'Identity' theft is defined as 'ID' theft, and occurs when a criminal uses fraudulently obtained personal information to obtain access to a card account in some else's name. There are two types: applying for an account in the name of another person or taking over an existing account.

2. Figures for ATM fraud and online banking fraud are not included in the total for some reason.

The figures are obtained from the following:

> *Card Fraud the Facts 2005* (APACS, 2005), for the years 1995 – 2005: page 5; the ATM fraud figures are taken from page 17
>
> *Card Fraud the Facts 2006* (APACS, 2006), for the years 1996 – 2005: page 5; the ATM fraud figures are taken from page 19
>
> *Card Fraud the Facts 2007* (APACS, 2007), for the years 1997 – 2006: page 5; the ATM fraud figures are taken from page 20
>
> *Card Fraud the Facts 2008* (APACS, 2008), for the years 1997 – 2007: page 6; the ATM fraud figures are taken from page 21
>
> *Card Fraud the Facts 2009* (APACS, 2009), for the years 1998 – 2006: page 5; the ATM fraud figures are taken from page 20
>
> *Fraud The Facts 2010* (Financial Fraud Action UK, 2010), for the years 1999 – 2009: page 7; the ATM fraud figures are taken from page 28
>
> *Fraud The Facts 2011* (Financial Fraud Action UK, 2011), for the years 2000 – 2010: page 7; the ATM fraud figures are taken from page 28
>
> *Fraud The Facts 2011* (Financial Fraud Action UK, 2012), for the years 2001 – 2011: page 7; the ATM fraud figures are taken from page 27
>
> *Fraud The Facts 2012* (Financial Fraud Action UK, 2012), for the years 2001 – 2011
>
> *Fraud The Facts 2013* (Financial Fraud Action UK, 2013), for the years 2002 – 2012: page 9; the ATM figures are taken from page 28

A missing figure

The number of people affected by fraud is under reported because of the reporting regime. Where the bank fails to reimburse the customer for a loss, and the police do not take action, the customer suffers the loss. It is this loss that is not recorded in any set of figures relating to financial fraud.

As indicated in 2009,[1] the fraud figures are probably greater than Financial Fraud Action UK would have us believe. This is of concern, because if the figures do not portray the losses incurred by customers accurately, the banking and credit card sector are in danger of believing their own propaganda that their information systems are as secure as they assert.

The Office for National Statistics publish an annual Report. The Report for 2013 is entitled: *Crime in England and Wales*, Year Ending June 2013 (17 October 2013). In this publication, the Office for National Statistics indicated that there were 299,547 reports of banking and payment related fraud.[2]

The Financial Services Ombudsman also publish a document entitled *Aggregate complaints statistics*.[3] In the publication covering 2006 to 2012, the figures for 2009 – 2012:

Number of complaints	Product group	2009-H1	2009-H2	2010-H1	2010-H2	2011-H1	2011-H2	2012-H1
Credit cards	Banking	171,481	195,082	203,131	235,712	227,511	248,911	330,098
Current accounts	Banking	588,876	1,627,310	634,959	474,429	395,757	370,595	323,955

(H1 means the first half of the year, H2 second half of the year)

Unfortunately, the figures given by the Financial Services Ombudsman are for all types of complaint, so it is difficult to know how many complaints dealt with ATM and online banking issues.

---

[1] Stephen Mason and Roger Porkess, 'Chip & pin fallacies' New Law Journal, Volume 159, No 7389, 16 October 2009, 1413-1414; Roger Porkess and Stephen Mason, 'Looking at debit and credit card fraud', *Teaching Statistics*, Volume 34, Number 3, Autumn 2012, 87 – 91.
[2] Available at http://www.ons.gov.uk/ons/dcp171778_331209.pdf.
[3] Available at http://www.financialombudsmanservice.net/publications/complaints-data.html.

Appendix 10

Debit cards, ATMs and negligence of the bank and customer

by Stephen Mason

This article was first published in *Butterworths Journal of International Banking and Financial Law*, Volume 27, Number 3, March 2012, 163 – 173

Key Points:
- Customers continue to suffer losses when using debit card "chip and pin" technology at ATMs that they ascribe to the fault of the bank.
- There are many instances where the bank uses its strength to ignore the failure of the security of its systems.
- The provision of secure and reliable banking systems must be the cornerstone of any duty that a bank owes its customer – and judges ought to take a robust view in favour of the customer where a bank fails to provide this.

Abstract:

There is little or no guidance from the courts as to what constitutes the negligent use of bank debit cards. This article considers the negligence of both the bank and the customer in relation to debit cards and ATMs. A distinction is made between duties surrounding the use of the cheque with that of "chip & pin" technology.

The introduction of 'chip & pin' technology to debit and credit cards in the United Kingdom was aimed at reducing the theft of cash, mainly through Automated Teller Machines (ATMs), by thieves that had worked out how to by-pass the security mechanisms put in place by the card issuers. This action was partly successful, although the figures have increased after a temporary reduction shortly after the introduction of the chip became effective. The rights and duties of the bank and the customer are generally determined by the terms and conditions that apply to the account, together with the provisions of the Payment Services Regulations 2009 (Statutory Instrument 2009 No. 209); this Statutory Instrument implements Directive 2007/64/EC of the European Parliament and of the Council of 13 November 2007 on payment services in the internal market amending Directives 97/7/EC, 2002/65/EC, 2005/60/EC and 2006/48/EC and repealing Directive 97/5/EC (Text with EEA relevance) OJ L319, 5.12.2007, p. 1–36. In the main, the contractual and legislative position significantly overlaps with any action in negligence that either the customer or the bank might have against the other.

There is little or no guidance from the courts as to what constitutes the negligent use of bank debit cards, and this article considers the negligence of both the bank and the customer in relation to debit cards and ATMs. Consideration is given to the duties of the customer and the bank, and what type of action or failure to act might be considered to be negligent in each case.

When determining if either the customer or the bank is negligent, it is necessary to consider whether the customer or bank acted negligently or omitted to do something they should have done, and if so, whether the loss sustained was the natural result of the negligence of the customer or the bank, or their failure to act. Whether there will be an effective remedy in damages is not considered.

The duties of the customer

The customer's contractual duties clearly overlap with any duty they may have in negligence. It is certainly the case that the customer owes a duty to the bank when writing a cheque to take reasonable and ordinary precautions against forgery. It must also be right that the customer also has a duty to take reasonable and ordinary precautions to prevent their card from being stolen or used by a thief.

The duty to protect against forgery

With a cheque, the customer is required to take reasonable precautions against forgery. But with a card and electronic signature (such as the PIN – a PIN is a form of electronic signature), it is difficult for the customer to prevent a thief from obtaining sufficient information from the legitimate card.

This means that if the bank insists on using technology that is inadequate or far from perfect, then the bank must take the consequences. The bank cannot take advantage of the weakness in the technology that customers are required to use; the flows of data through a number of third parties; the failure of employees that are responsible for the technology; and the failure to fully control the complex sub-contracting that takes place within the industry.

The bank cannot complain of the consequences of their own default against customers who are misled by those very defaults of technology and the failure to obey operating manuals.

The distinction between the cheque, and the card and a PIN lies in the manner in which the two items are used and the ease by which a perfect forgery is possible with the card and a PIN. The customer has more control when writing out a cheque, but the crucial difference between the cheque and the card and the PIN is that the card and PIN can only be considered to be in the relative safe keeping of the customer, and when the card is used, it is exposed to the weaknesses of the technology.

The customer is at the mercy of unknown unknowns. It is the bank that is aware of many of these unknown unknowns because they are internal to the bank, but the banks are also prey to their own unknown unknowns, yet the sector refuses to acknowledge the weaknesses in the technology. Indeed, as the criminal cases noted below illustrate, there have been (and probably continue to be) significant failures in the technology used by the banks.

A further discussion in relation to the intervention of a crime is considered below under the rubric 'where the intervention of an intervening crime causes loss'.

The PIN

The bank will include a number of contractual duties relating to the PIN in the contract with the customer that include the following:

> To take all reasonable steps to keep the PIN secret at all times.
>
> To take every care to stop anyone else using the PIN.
>
> To destroy the piece of paper the bank sends with a record of the PIN.
>
> Not to write the PIN on the card or anything else usually kept with the card.

Customers are at a disadvantage when using the technology. The first disadvantage is that the bank makes it a requirement that the customer must use the technology, so the customer rarely has a choice about accepting and using a card. Second, there are many methods that thieves can use to obtain the PIN, the information stored on the magnetic strip of the card without the knowledge of the customer, and the card itself, as noted below. By using the magnetic strip only, banks in countries such as the United States of America have demonstrated an unwillingness to take reasonable precautions to protect their customers by introducing a chip. While the addition of a chip is not guaranteed to prevent thieves, it does act as a more effective barrier.

For this reason, a judge will have to decide what the 'reasonable steps' are that a customer must take to keep the PIN secret, and what the customer must do to 'take every care' to prevent anyone else using the PIN. It is unlikely that there will be any defined set of guidance produced by judges, because the facts in each case are different.

The duty of the customer not to reveal the PIN

It must be right that where a customer gives out the PIN to another person, whether it is a family member or a thief, the customer will, depending on the facts, have acted negligently, and will be prevented from claiming that they were not negligent. If the customer is disabled or not able to use the card and PIN because of their age or some other infirmity, it is possible not to be considered negligent where the PIN is given to a third party that is authorised to act on behalf of the customer. In such circumstances, the bank should be made aware of such an arrangement, and be given information about the person with the authority to act for the customer. Where a third party acts on behalf of the customer, the duties that bind the customer will also bind the authorised third party.

When assessors at the Financial Ombudsman Service consider complaints, reliance is placed on the guidance set out in the *Electronic Funds Transfer Code of Conduct* (as revised by the Australian Securities and Investments Commission's EFT Working Group) (Issued 1 April 2001 Amended 18 March 2002 and 1 November 2008). Although a customer might not be aware of this Code of Conduct, there should not be a difference between what is covered in the Code and the terms and conditions of the bank.

In assessing whether a customer has contributed to losses by writing down the PIN or any other code, the following principles will apply, as set out in the *Banking & Finance Policies and Procedures Manual (Extract dealing with Credit Card Disputes and Electronic Funds Transfer Investigations)* (Financial Ombudsman Service, 2008). These

principles will also apply to any device used for on-line banking:
A user may keep a record of the PIN.

> The PIN should not be written on the card.

> The customer should make a reasonable attempt to protect the PIN.

> If the PIN is not reasonably protected, it must not be carried with the card, or kept in such a way that it could be lost or stolen with the card.

Protecting the PIN comprises two aspects: that of disguising the PIN in a reasonable way, and taking reasonable steps to prevent the PIN from being obtained without authority.

Where a PIN or password is chosen by the customer, it is important to ensure that it is not easy to guess. For this reason, the Financial Ombudsman Service has indicated that a customer will usually be in breach of the principles where the customer decides on a PIN that represents their date of birth or is a part of their name that is easy to recognise.

Disguising the PIN

In *Banking & Finance Policies and Procedures Manual*, the Financial Ombudsman Service offer some advice as to what a customer can do to conceal or disguise the PIN or password. They include:

> Re-arranging the numerals or letters that the bank has provided, and substituting other numbers, letters or symbols.

> Concealing the PIN or password by:
>
>> making it appear as another type of number or word, or surrounding the PIN or password with other numerals, letters or symbols
>>
>> placing the PIN or password in a location or context where it would not be expected to be found, such as on a piece of paper in a cookery book
>>
>> using a combination of all of these approaches

Whether the disguise of the PIN is reasonable

Where a PIN or password has been disguised, the problem might be that the method used by the customer has not been effective. The Financial Ombudsman Service has indicated that the attempt to disguise the PIN does not have to be the most reasonable that could have been used. The method of disguising the PIN might not have been successful, but the lack of success does not make the attempt to disguise it unreasonable. How reasonable the disguise was will be considered on its merits, and each case must be taken individually.

In considering whether the attempt to disguise was reasonable, an assessment will be made from the point of the reasonable user that is a person:

>of average intelligence

>who does not have the knowledge and experience of a thief or bank claims officer about the strengths and weaknesses of different types of disguises

>who has sufficient, but not specialised, computer skills when it comes to using banking facilities

>who is aware of widely publicised warnings by their bank and the Ombudsman about unsafe methods to disguise a PIN

If a PIN is disguised in a way that a thief can easily find it, it is more likely that the customer will be considered to be negligent. Examples provided by the Ombudsman include:

>Recording the PIN as a series of numbers with any of them marked, circled or highlighted to indicate what the PIN is.

>Recording the PIN in such a way that it stands out as a PIN, for example where the PIN is recorded as a four digit 'telephone number' when all the other telephone numbers are eight digit numbers.

>Recording the PIN in isolation from other information.

>Recording the PIN as a birth date, postcode or telephone number without the benefit of a further element of disguise.

Ways in which a customer might be considered to be negligent

There has not been any case law in England & Wales to provide a list of examples about what might be considered to be negligent, but a number of cases in Germany provide some guidance. The list below is from the German cases (taken from Assistant Professor DDr. Gerwin Haybäck, 'Civil law liability for unauthorized withdrawals at ATMs in Germany' *Digital Evidence and Electronic Signature Law Review*, 6 (2009) 57 – 66). It is possible that judges in England & Wales might reach different decisions because of different facts. Nevertheless customers might be considered to be negligent in the following circumstances:

(i) By keeping a written note of the PIN in an address book together with the card.

(ii) Where the customer places bank statements and the card carelessly into the pocket of a coat or jacket.

(iii) If the customer leaves their flat for three or four hours and leaves the card and the PIN on the desk in their flat, or if the customer keeps the card and the PIN in a folder.

(iv) Keeping the card with the PIN (as a four-digit telephone number) together in a solid strong box in a locked sick room in a hospital.

(v) Where a purse containing the customer's card is placed in a shopping trolley in a department store.

The customer is also urged to shield the reader of a terminal when they key in their PIN. The value of such shields (when provided) is doubtful, given the wide variety of terminal designs, the location of terminals and how easy it is for others to observe the customer typing in their PIN.

It must also be right that even though the customer has a contractual duty to inform the bank of any circumstances that lead them to think that their card or PIN has been compromised in any way, nevertheless, failing to alert the bank immediately that they are aware that something might be wrong must also be considered to be a negligent act of omission.

Where the intervention of an intervening crime causes loss

A customer is not negligent where a criminal act for which they are not responsible intervenes between them and any loss they might suffer. With respect to cards and electronic signatures (PINs), this aspect has the greatest resonance in the twenty-first century.

The negligence of the customer and the effect of an intervening act was the topic of discussion in *London Joint Stock Bank v Macmillan* [1918] AC 777, in which a clerk presented a cheque drawn in favour of the firm or bearer, in the sum of £2.0.0 to a partner for signature. The partner was in a rush, and signed the cheque. Only the amount in figures was filled in, not the amount in words. The clerk subsequently added the words 'one hundred and twenty pounds' in the space left for the words and added the figures '1' and '0' respectively each side of the figure '2'. The clerk subsequently presented the cheque for payment and was never seen again. The firm took action against the bank to recover the money, without success.

In his argument before the members of the House of Lords, Holman Gregory QC for Macmillan and Arthur, the respondents, indicated the issue at 785:

> 'If a customer by his act or omission misleads the bank, and loss is sustained as the natural result of that act or omission, the customer is responsible for that loss. It is not necessary to quarrel with that principle. That involves two questions of fact: 1. Was there a negligent act or omission by the customer? 2. Was the loss sustained as the natural result thereof?'

It was argued without success at 786 that 'It was not the form in which the drawer drew the cheque which misled the banker, but the intervening crime....' and 'At any rate, the intervention of a crime is an important factor in determining whether the customer has been guilty of negligence.'

Lord Finlay LC considered whether the intervention of a crime acts to make a forgery too remote, and in the case he was providing a judgment upon, he was correct. However, his comment, at 811, if considered in relation to cards and electronic signatures, has a significantly different meaning:

> 'Indeed, forgery is the very thing against which the customer is bound to take reasonable precautions.'

With a cheque, this indeed is the case. But with a card and electronic signature, the opposite must be the case. The customer is not in a position to take reasonable steps against forgery, unless they never use their card and electronic signature (and even this is risky, as the case of *United States v. Albert Gonzalez* (08-CR-10223, 09-CR-10262, 09-CR-10382, http://www.justice.gov/usao/ma/news/IDTheft/gonzalez.html) illustrates, for the risks of a thief obtaining sufficient information to forge a card and electronic signature have been with us since the invention of the cards, and as the technology changes, so the methods of attack will continue to alter and adapt. In fact, Lord Finlay LC accepted, at 811, that:

> 'No one can be certain of preventing forgery, but it is a very simple thing in drawing a cheque to take reasonable and ordinary precautions against forgery.'

Arguably, Lord Finlay LC was correct in respect of a cheque, but could not envisage the technology that the banking industry was to initiate some fifty-five years after he made these comments. It is now very difficult for a customer to take reasonable and ordinary precautions against forgery – in many ways, the need for the banks to produce adequate evidence to prove the customer was the person at the ATM withdrawing the cash is even greater now than with previous methods of moving money, such as the cheque. The fact is, that the perfect forgery is possible with cards and electronic signatures. In fact, Lord Finlay LC observed, at 812, how the cheque in question in the case before the House of Lords appeared to be a perfect forgery:

> 'The examination of the facsimile of the cheque when filled up shows how impossible it was to detect the fraud.'

Thus it is with cards and electronic signatures as a matter of course. In this respect, Lord Finlay LC (at 796) quoted the remarks made by Cleasby B in the case of *The Guardians of Halifax Union v Wheelwright* (1873-74) 9 – 10 L.R.Exch. 183 at 192, which have a resonance to the modern world of banking technology as ever they did when he wrote them:

> 'a man cannot take advantage of his own wrong, a man cannot complain of the consequences of his own default, against a person who was misled by that default without any fault of his own'

This is also a point noted by Viscount Haldene, at 816:

> 'the banker as a mandatory has a right to insist on having his mandate in a form which does not leave room for misgiving as to what he is called on to do,'

Although this is a cheque case, nevertheless the discussions by their Lordships help to place the technology used by the banks into context. When dealing with different forms of technology, additional considerations must apply. The first question of fact remains, although the complexity of the technology does not necessarily make this an easy question to answer: 'Was there a negligent act or omission by the customer?' Where it is determined that the first question shows that there was a negligent act or omission by the customer, the second question follows: 'Was the loss sustained as the natural result thereof?'

The first point of discussion is whether 'the customer knows that a forged cheque is in circulation and neglects to notify the bank'. Consider the various possibilities in relation to the technology of modern cards:

> (i) First, the customer is aware of, and authorises others to use their card and electronic signature. In such a case, the customer might give each person a right, under given circumstances, to use the card and electronic signature on behalf of the customer. Where the customer's bank is aware of such an arrangement in advance, it might be that the bank will issue a second card to the authorised party, and then any transactions carried out by the authorised party will be undertaken under the terms of agency as between the authorised party and the customer of the bank. In circumstances where the authorised person goes beyond the authority extended to them by the customer, the customer will take the loss. Where the arrangement is less formal, and the bank is not aware of such an arrangement, the risk lies with the customer for any misuse of the card until such time as the customer informs the bank and requests the cancellation of the card, for instance. In both cases, where a person is authorised directly or implicitly to use the card and electronic signature, and goes beyond the mandate (whether the mandate is formal or informal), then a crime is being committed. In these circumstances, whether the customer has been negligent will turn on the precise facts of each case. The customer issued a

mandate, and it is for the customer to ensure the mandate is not breached – that is, unless the technical weaknesses are such that money is withdrawn from the customer's account and neither the customer nor the authorised users of the card are responsible for the loss.

(ii) Second, the customer deals with their card in such a way that they know others will be able to find and use the card, and third parties know the customer has also written the electronic signature on or near the card, or the electronic signature is a sequence of numbers that are so closely associated with the customer that the customer will always use this particular sequence, or it is notorious as to where the customer keeps their electronic signature.

(iii) Finally, the customer may have taken great care to provide for the safety of their card and electronic signature, but in despite of this, a third party, possibly a close relative, obtains the card and electronic signature. Depending on the circumstances, the customer is generally not held to be grossly negligent. (These scenarios and the consequences are similar to the seal cases, for which, see Stephen Mason, *Electronic Signatures in Law,* chapter 1).

Now compare this proposition with the technology of the chip and pin card and the position a customer might find themselves in: Where the customer has knowledge that their card might be compromised, the customer has a duty to notify the bank immediately. For the customer to be liable, it is necessary to establish how and when the customer might become aware that their card was compromised. However, a customer is rarely aware that a forged card is circulating amongst thieves until they receive their monthly statement, or they check their balance and find the account denuded, or they wish to use their banking facilities to discover there are no funds available. The technology imposed on customers by the banks is such that a forged card and a forged electronic signature can be used minutes after a successful cloning of the card, or after the magnetic stripe has been skimmed and the electronic signature observed.

In this respect, the comments of Lord Finlay LC, at 795 no longer remain quite as true in respect of card technology: 'Of course the negligence must be in the transaction itself, that is, in the manner in which the cheque is drawn.'

A second point to consider is the comment that 'the intervention of a crime is an important factor in determining whether the customer has been guilty of negligence.' With respect to cards and electronic signatures, this aspect of the argument used by Holman Gregory QC has the greatest significance in the twenty-first century. The distinction between the cheque, and the card and electronic signature lies in the manner in which the two items are used and the ease by which a perfect forgery is possible with the latter. Lord Finlay LC observed, at 809 that 'the manner in which the cheque is to be filled up is entirely in the hands of the customer'.

The crucial difference between the cheque and the card and electronic signature is that the card and electronic signature can only be considered to be in the relative safe keeping of the customer, and when the card is used, it is exposed to the weaknesses of the technology used by the banks. A card can apparently be 'swallowed' by an ATM, and a thief can persuade the customer to think the ATM has taken the card, and subsequently retrieve the card when the customer has left the scene. The thief can then have a cloned version operating in seconds on the streets of a city thousands of miles away. The banks require customers to use technology that is imperfect, although they may claim otherwise – indeed, they have consistently claimed otherwise for many years, and yet the technology they use is continually demonstrated to be at fault.

Where the thief obtains the card, or the data, or the PIN (or all of these) from the customer

It is relatively easy for a third party to obtain the electronic signature and the details of the account in the magnetic stripe of the card without the knowledge of the card holder, (as a starting point, the reader is directed to Ross J. Anderson, *Security Engineering* (2nd edn, Wiley, 2008)) and a thief can even obtain the original card by deception or by intercepting it as it is sent from the bank to the customer by post, together with the electronic signature. This is the first point of attack on the technology that the banks make their customers use. The customer cannot be responsible for failing to deal with such risks.

Often, it will not be known how the PIN was obtained, and it will be for the judge to determine, based on the evidence before her, whether the bank has proven its case that it was the customer. For instance, in 1980, Dorothy Judd discovered two withdrawals were made from her account by use of a cash card and PIN in the sum of US$800 (*Judd v Citibank*, N.Y.City Civ.Ct., 435 N.Y.S.2d 210). At the material time she was at her place of employment, and her employer corroborated her evidence by writing a letter to confirm her presence at her place of work. Citibank produced computer print-outs setting out the details of the withdrawals in issue, the content of which was explained by the branch manager. It appears from the report that the bank merely asserted, by way of a statement in support, that the security measures in place to prevent the unauthorised use of cash cards was so stringent as to prevent the possibility of a PIN from being used other than by the person whose number it was. Marmarellis J indicated that the case turned on issues of evidence, burden and credibility. In his judgment, the learned judge referred to the lack of expert qualifications of the manager, but not the evidentiary foundations of the statement from the bank, in which the soundness of the security system in place was asserted. He determined the issue by considering whether the plaintiff had proven her case by a fair preponderance of the credible evidence. In this instance, the issue was whether to believe the person or the machine. In reaching a decision, Marmarellis, J referred to the 1977 Report to the Congress *EFT in the United States, Final Report of the National Commission on Electronic Fund Transfers* (National Commission on Electronic Fund Transfers, Washington, D.C., October 1977) and recommendation 5, which reads:

> 'If the depository institution denies the alleged error or its responsibility for the error or unauthorized use, the customer should have the burden of initiating any further proceeding, such as a lawsuit, to establish his right to have his account credited or recredited. Once a lawsuit has been initiated by a depositor, the depository institution has the burden to prove that there was no error or unauthorized use for which it was responsible.'

The learned judge commented that the recommendations of the Commission were not law, and looked forward to legislation dealing with the issue. (The Electronic Fund Transfer Act (15 U.S.C. 1693 was passed in 1978 and the Electronic Code of Federal Regulations, Part 205 – Electronic Fund Transfer (Regulation E) applies to cash cards.) He decided not to apply the recommendations of the Commission, but commented, at 212:

> '... this court is not prepared to go so far as to rule that where a credible witness is faced with the adverse "testimony" of a

machine, he is as a matter of law faced also with an unmeetable burden of proof. It is too commonplace in our society that when faced with the choice of man or machine we readily accept the "word" of the machine every time. This, despite the tales of computer malfunctions that we hear daily. [The] defendant's own witness testified to physical malfunction of the very system in issue.'

Marmarellis J determined that the plaintiff proved her case 'by a fair preponderance of the credible evidence' and judgment was awarded in the amount of the loss plus interest and disbursements. Two further cases followed in 1981 (*Feldman v. Citibank, N.A.,; Pickman v. Citibank, N.A*, N.Y.City Civ.Ct., 443 N.Y.S.2d 43) but it was the case of *Ognibene v. Citibank, N.A.*, N.Y.City Civ.Ct., 446 N.Y.S.2d 845 that is of interest in the context of this article, in which the judge took judicial notice of news reports in the media of a number of methods used by thieves to steal money from ATMs, including where money was stolen by deceiving the customer into cooperating with the thief.

The case of *Ognibene* is a useful reminder that the customer cannot be responsible for failing to deal with such risks. It must be for the bank to prove that the customer was not the subject of such an attack.

Criminals also obtain the confidential data held on debit cards from unsuspecting individuals with the specific intention of transferring the data to false cards in order to use ATMs to withdraw funds. A variety of methods are employed to obtain sufficient information from a card to use it to steal money, such as copying the data stored on the magnetic stripe on a card as it is used in the ATM, where a small electronic camera is mounted above the key pad of the cash machine, so it records the PIN being used, and a card reader is placed over the legitimate slot for the card, and the data is read simultaneously by the false reader, as described in the following cases: England & Wales *R v Cenan (Sebastian)* [2004] ECWA Crim 3388; 2004 WL 3255240 (CA (Crim Div)), *R v Chirila (Remus Tenistocle)* [2005] 1 Cr.App.R.(S.) 92; [2004] EWCA Crim 2200, *R v Dabijia (Catalin Ionut)* [2005] EWCA Crim 318; 2005 WL 588736 (CA (Crim Div)); Canada: *R v Ciocata* [2004] A.J. No. 207; 2004 ABPC 39.

Another methodology is described in the Singapore case of *Public Prosecutor v Meng* [2006] SGDC 243 involving defendants of an organised syndicate based in West Malaysia. This enabled thieves to collect details on the card numbers and the PIN before producing cloned cards.

The wide availability of small card scanners enables a card to be skimmed, which enables the thief to produce a cloned version of the card, (as described in *R v Taj, R v Gardner, R v Samuel* [2003] EWCA Crim 2633; 2003 WL 22257755, *R v Wong (Kok Kee)* [2004] EWCA Crim 1170; 2004 WL 1060608 (CA (Crim Div), *Attorney General's Reference No. 73 of 2003 (Umaharan Ranganathan)* [2004] 2 Cr.App. R.(S.) 62; [2004] EWCA Crim 183; 2004 WL 229130, *R v Din (Ameen)* [2005] 2 Cr.App.R.(S.) 40; [2004] EWCA Crim 3364; 2004 WL 3131381; for Canada see *R v Coman* [2004] A.J. No 383; 2004 ABPC 18, *R v Naqvi* [2005] A.J. No 1593; 2005 ABPC 339, *R v Mayer* 2006 ABPC 30 for Singapore see *Balasingam v Public Prosecutor* [2006] SGHC 228) especially in restaurants and retail outlets, although the attacker may obtain the PIN by just watching the victim type the numbers into a key pad before stealing the card when the opportunity arises, for which see the New Zealand case of *R v Telea* Court of Appeal, CA396/00, 4 December 2000, Keith, Blanchard and Tipping JJ. Other methods to obtain a PIN include the use of a mobile telephone to take photographs, or the video facility to capture the PIN being used on a key pad, or the use of x-ray film to trap the card in the ATM, so after the victim fails to recover their card, the thief quickly returns to the ATM and recovers the legitimate card, having obtained the PIN.

In any event, the crime can be lucrative. For instance, in *R v Mayer* 2006 ABCA 149 (CANLII); 2006 ABPC 30 a group of thieves stole over C$1m in undertaking such activities. Not all problems with ATMs are the result of attacks by criminals: the banks themselves may be put into a position where they are required to admit that they have problems, such as the failure for ATMs to balance, as in *Porter v Citibank N.A.*, 123 Misc.2d 28, 472 N.Y.S.2D 582, where an employee of the bank admitted that, on average, the cash machines were out of balance once or twice a week. Also, simple attacks can be equally as effective, such as theft of the card and PIN before it reaches the customer, for which see in India, *Bharteeya v The State* 121(2005) DLT 369; 2005 (83) DRJ 299; and England & Wales: *R v Molcher (Andrew Alan)* [2006] EWCA Crim 1522; 2006 WL 2049662 (CA (Crim Div)).

The negligence of the bank
There are a variety of ways in which a bank can be considered to be negligent in undertaking its duties towards its customers, many of which are noted in the discussion above by implication. In broad

terms, for the customer to raise the issue, it will be necessary to challenge the efficiency of the security mechanisms put in place by the bank or offer a credible alternative explanation for what happened.

The failure of the ATM and back end banking systems

The customer relies upon the hardware and software put in place by the bank and any third parties contracted with the bank to provide services within the payment infrastructure. Even such an innocuous series of transactions involving an ATM may well involve an ATM owned by a third party and rented out to another party, the telephone line to the bank may be controlled by yet another party, who may be responsible for the security; a database link may well exist between VocaLink (VocaLink was created on 2 July 2007 from the combination of Voca and LINK Interchange Network) or some other third party, and a facilities management company may well be a link in the chain between VocaLink and the issuing bank. For this reason, the customer is totally reliant on the security, integrity and robust nature of the systems in place, together with the assessments of the systems, the results of internal audits, external audits, and audits by insurers. None of this information is made available to the customer, so the customer has to have complete trust in the integrity and reliability of such systems and the ability of the banks to identify and prevent insider fraud taking place. Note also the United States case of *United States v. Albert Gonzalez*, in which Gonzalez and others obtained unauthorised access to networks over wireless networks that processed and stored credit card and debit card transactions, and then obtained files containing data and encrypted PIN blocks. The importance of this case cannot be emphasised too much, bearing in mind that the PIN should never be released to anybody, yet this case demonstrates that some card issuers apparently seem to be treating the security of PINs somewhat indifferently.

An example of where it is probable that such a breakdown occurred is in a case before Seneka J of the Papua New Guinea District Court, *Roni v Kagure* [2004] PGDC 1; DC84 (1 January 2004). The learned judge found for Mathew Roni against the Bank of South Pacific. Mr Roni discovered the loss of his Save Card, and informed the bank immediately he knew of the loss. It was not in dispute that the bank put a stop to all withdrawals on 21 October 2002 at 10 am. It subsequently transpired that a number of transactions occurred after 10 am, and the bank looked to Mr Roni to compensate them for the withdrawals. The evidence demonstrated that a number of withdrawals took place simultaneously at different locations, as described by Seneka J:

> 'How could the person who stole [the] complainant's Save Card on 18/10/02 withdraw K1000.00 from Mt. Hagen by 06:04 am on 21/10/02 and another K1000.00 from Goroka at 6:16 am [on the] same date. Then within 1 ½ hours later in Goroka at Bintangor and Best Buy used the card for K884.05. At about 8:30 am [the] same date withdraw K1000.00 from BSP Mt. Hagen. Defendant has no explanation nor raised any to these transactions.'

In this instance, the learned judge reached the conclusion that the bank was negligent. The report of the case does not indicate whether the card was lost with the PIN, but two separate ATMs were used to obtain access to and remove cash from the same account in two separate physical locations at roughly the same time.

The problem with cases of this nature, is that the evidence provided by the banks tends to assert their systems are perfect, and therefore they are not at fault. That this line of reasoning is unreliable can be observed from the case of Maxwell Parsons, who used an MP3 player to obtain details of cards as they were used in free standing ATMs. He entered a plea of guilty at Minshull Street Crown Court in Manchester in November 2006 to possessing equipment to make a false instrument, deception and unlawful interception of a public telecommunication transmission. He was sentenced to 32 months in prison. He, together with others, stole up to £200,000 from free standing ATMs. Reports in the media explained how it worked (Russell Jenkins, 'Hole-in-wall thief used MP3 player,' *The Times*, 15 November 2006): The telephone line that connects the ATM to a BT line was disconnected, and a two-way adaptor inserted. The MP3 player was then placed between the ATM output cable and the telephone socket. The MP3 player recorded the tones sent over the telephone line, and the data was subsequently converted to readable numbers using a separate computer programme, and added to cloned cards, which in turn were used to steal by buying goods using the legitimate data. The police were made aware of the scheme by accident when they stopped Parsons for a motoring offence in London. They found a false bank card in his possession, and after searching his home in Manchester, they discovered technical equipment necessary to carry out the swindle, together with 26 bank cards, 18 of which were cloned. As this prosecution indicates, it is clearly beyond the ability of the customer to exercise any control over their PIN, whether the card and PIN remains in their possession or not.

Lax banking controls

Other problems highlight the significance of this issue, in that the banks themselves are also partly to blame for the failure of their systems. An example of the sloppy controls that can become apparent with respect to ATMs is illustrated in the case of *Patty v Commonwealth Bank of Australia* Industrial Relations Court of Australia VI-2542 of 1996; [2000] FCA 1072. In this instance, A$27,400 was stolen from an ATM machine. The police investigated the complaint made by the bank, but reached the conclusion that there was insufficient evidence to prosecute. (Compare this with *Windebank v Pryce* [2001] NTSC 45, where the investigation was woefully inadequate). The bank subsequently continued to investigate the theft, and eventually dismissed Mr Patty. Of relevance are the findings of fact by the Judicial Registrar, none of which were significantly challenged in the subsequent application to review the decision. The findings of fact illustrate the slack nature of the controls that can exist within a bank respecting the security of ATMs. First, it is helpful to describe how the ATMs were serviced. The learned Judicial Registrar described the system as follows (there are neither page numbers nor paragraph numbers in the internet version of this judgment):

> 'ATM machines are usually accessed by removing two combinations, a top combination known as the 'A' combination or lock and the bottom combination known as the 'B' combination or lock. ATM service teams usually comprise two officers. The teams are rostered to attend to operational faults out of hours and especially to attend to these faults at weekends. Machine malfunction is common. Many operational faults are fixed by ATM service teams. The usual procedure involves each member of the team being responsible for calculating and removing either the A or B combination on the ATM. Each team member is issued with a sealed envelope which contains numbers which allow for the calculation of either the A or B combination.'

The events that occurred before the theft, together with the nature of the controls put in place by the bank, are taken from the judgment and merit setting out in detail below to illustrate the nature of the problem and the issues that can arise:

'At 13.43.39.04 (i.e. at 1.43 pm) Centofanti logged on with the Voice Response Unit (VRU) in Sydney. He did this by telephone from the Collingwood Service Centre at 150 Smith Street. Very soon thereafter, the applicant contacted the Security Monitoring Centre (SMC) and advised that the service team was in the branch and was about to deactivate the alarm system. There are log reports provided by SMC and Wormald Security Monitoring Service confirming these logging on calls.

Centofanti attempted to obtain the B combination for the ATM by using a touch phone and keying in his staff number and (supposedly) the bank branch number. At about 13.45.33.04 (i.e. at 1.45 pm) Centofanti keyed in an incorrect branch number and could not further access a series of numbers which, if obtained, and deducted from other numbers held by him in a sealed envelope, would have provided the correct combination for the B lock on the ATM machine.

At this stage, the applicant went downstairs. He has stated that he went downstairs to use the toilet. Meanwhile, Centofanti, having failed to obtain the B combination because of an invalid branch number, attempted to contact two other bank officers by phone with a view to obtaining the correct branch number and accessing it. He was unsuccessful in locating either bank officer and began searching desk drawers in the hope of locating the correct branch number. He located a grey key card wallet in the top drawer on the left hand side of a desk normally occupied by the second in charge of the bank. Centofanti described the wallet as 'old and tatty'. Within the wallet, on a 'Record of Account Details Card', two series of numbers were written. He assumed that the numbers might have been the actual combinations of the A and B locks for the ATM. He was correct in the assumption that one series of numbers represented the A combination. Using these numbers he removed the A combination. Using the other series of numbers, he unsuccessfully tried to remove the B combination. The applicant had by then returned from downstairs. Centofanti asked the applicant to try and remove the B combination using the numbers on the card. The applicant tried and was also unsuccessful.

The Court pauses to note that the recording of ATM combination numbers and the leaving of such numbers in any place where access might be obtained was a clear breach of the respondent's security procedures. This was only one of many breaches of security procedures which occurred at 150 Smith Street and which appear to have occurred frequently at many branches of the bank. On that day Centofanti was responsible for the B combination. His removal of the A combination was a breach of security procedure. The applicant was responsible for the A combination. His attempts to remove the B combination were also a breach of security procedure.

At this stage, Centofanti successfully contacted another ATM service member by telephone and obtained from her the correct branch number. While Centofanti was so engaged, the applicant continued to search desk drawers in the hope of locating the B combination.

Once Centofanti had obtained the branch number he logged on again with VRU by touch phone and was placed on hold. At weekends, service team members often have to wait to be provided with numbers which allow calculation of combination locks. Such relatively short delays appear to be an inevitable result of the volume of telephone calls made by service team members. While Centofanti was on hold, the applicant successfully 'solved' the ATM 'communication problem' by resetting a controller or rebooting a modem.

While the applicant was so engaged, Centofanti obtained the appropriate numbers from VRU and calculated the B combination which he wrote on 'a piece of paper'. Although the ATM communication problem appeared solved because of the applicant's resetting of a controller, Centofanti decided to open the ATM and confirm the machine was working by performing what is known as a 'COCO' test. To perform the COCO test, having earlier removed the A combination, he removed the B combination using the combination number on the piece of paper, partially opened the ATM security door and flicked a toggle switch located inside the ATM security area. The ATM then performed a self test program which registered a 'COCO display' which indicated that the machine was once more in working order. Centofanti then secured the ATM door by spinning the combinations and telephoned VRU to log on for the next service call. At the same time, the applicant advised SMC that the alarm was about to be reactivated.'

The banks, by various mechanisms, force their customers to use technology, yet the very systems upon which they rely are not always as robust as they could be. As Professor Anderson illustrates in his text, the systems put in place by banks are not as secure as some maintain. For instance, it was demonstrated that it was possible for an attacker in the bank to discover approximately 7,000 PINs relatively quickly (Mike Bond and Piotr Zieliński, 'Decimalisation table attacks for PIN cracking' Technical Report Number 560 (February 2003, Computer Laboratory UCAM-CL-TR-560)), and known weaknesses in standards that may be responsible for unauthorised withdrawals have not been addressed by the banks.

Additionally, the processing system used by banks is open to abuse. One method is to attack the translate function in switches, and another makes use of the functions that are used to allow customers to select a new PIN on-line. In both instances, the flaws enable an attacker, if they have access to the on-line PIN verification facility or switching processes, to discover PINs, such as those entered by customers while withdrawing cash from an ATM (for which, see Omer Berkman and Odelia Moshe Ostrovsky, 'The unbearable lightness of PIN cracking,' available on-line at http:// www.arx.com/documents/ The_Unbearable_Lightness_of_PIN_Cracking.pdf. For information about different types of attack on ATMs in the past, see Ann All, 'ATM History Industry 2002: A year in view' 7 January 2003 on-line at http://www.atmmarketplace.com/article.php?id=3281).

Insider theft

Thefts also take place entirely from within the bank, for which see *United States of America v Bonallo*, 858 F.2d 1427 (9th Cir. 1988); *Kumar v Westpac Banking Corporation* [2001] FJHC 159; *Sefo v R* [2004] TOSC 51 and *R v Clarke* [2005] QCA 483. See *Windebank v Pryce* [2001] NTSC 45 for a discussion of 'Night and Day' cards, and the inadequate safeguards in place within a bank branch respecting the PIN, and lax controls over logging on to computers by members of staff.

The problem is not always the failure of the bank ATM system, but in the procedural system employed to issue cards of a similar nature, such as electronic benefit transfer cards issued by the Retirement and Disability unit of the Penrith office of Centrelink described in *R v Thompson* [2002] NSWCCA 149), although attempts at stealing large sums of money tends to be conducted with help from a mixture of the slipshod controls within the bank itself, together with somebody working on the inside of the bank, as illustrated in the cases of *In the matter of Adeniyi Momodu Allison v Bow Street Magistrates' Court ex parte Adeniyi Momodu Allison, R v* [1998] EWHC Admin 536, in which it was alleged that Joan Ojomo, a credit card analyst, supplied account information to her external co-conspirators, who were then able to obtain a PIN or replacement PIN to draw cash from ATMs, and *R v Stephen Edward Seaton* [1998] EWCA Crim 754, the details of which are described by the Vice President:

> 'The applicant and the others conspired to obtain money from automated teller machines, referred to as ATMs, by the use of counterfeit credit and cash cards. They planned to enter British Telecom exchanges with the assistance of corrupted employees of that organisation, in order to gain access to lines passing from ATMs to the mainframe computers. Taps and memory boards were placed on those lines, and used to record details of the cards of account holders while they were being transmitted down the lines. Those details recorded in that way were then to be downloaded onto a computer, and decrypted.
>
> The information obtained by that means was then to be transferred, using a read/write machine, onto blank plastic cards obtained for the purpose. The blank cards thus informed could then be used at ATMs to withdraw money.
>
> The applicant played a major role in this conspiracy. He had a list of door code keys for every telephone exchange within the M25 area, and he said those had been obtained from a BT engineer. The coaccused, Moore, was in charge of the computer program. The coaccused, Haward, owned premises which constituted the main operational base for the conspirators.'

In another case, that of *R v Stubbs* [2006] EWCA Crim 2312, a clerk, a member of a password reset team (comprising two people), was involved in fraudulent money transfers from the HSBC Bank between 23 July and 27 July 2002. In this case, four attempts were made to transfer money from corporate clients of the bank using an on-line banking system called 'Hexagon'. A fifth attempt, against the account of AT&T Wireless, succeeded. Three money transfers, each of about £1.9m, were made from the AT&T account on 25 July to an account held with Barclays Bank in Leicester in the name of Advanced New Technologies Corporation Ltd. The deposit was then converted into euros before being transferred to the account of a company registered in Spain, trading as Vasat Importacion SL in Madrid. A further transfer of £6.1m was effected on 26 July from the AT&T account to the same recipients. None of the money removed from the AT&T account was recovered.

Note also the Canadian case of *R v Brum* [1999] O.J. No. 4727; [2001] O.J. No. 1731 in which the appellant was alleged to be in possession of both the upper and lower combination sets of access codes used to service ATMs, but the members of the Court of Appeal agreed that the evidence was not sufficient, and ordered a new trial.

The duties of the bank

A useful source of information that helps to reinforce the duties expected of the banks as set out in the Financial Services Authority book *Banking: Conduct of Business sourcebook*, is a guide written by the British Bankers' Association, the Building Societies Association and the Payments Council for its members in January 2011 with the title *Industry Guidance for FSA Banking Conduct of Business Sourcebook*. Although any rights that may accrue under the provisions of the *Banking: Conduct of Business sourcebook* and section 150 of the Financial Services and Markets Act 2000 might be narrowly defined, nevertheless it is arguable that the provisions set out in *Industry Guidance* ought to be considered in a wider context, given that the document recognises that banks have significant duties to perform. Two sections are particularly relevant, in the light of the comment in the introduction that states 'Firms regulated by the FSA must also comply with the FSA's Principles for Businesses'. The introduction to section 5 provides the following:

'Section 5: Post sale requirements

5.1 Introduction

Chapter 5 of BCOBS sets out rules relating to the way in which a firm must treat a customer after they enter into a contract for a product or service. Firms must act promptly, fairly and efficiently when providing retail banking services.

The way that firms deal with customers post sale is important in achieving the desired outcomes for Treating Customers Fairly under FSA's Principle 6. In particular firms should have regard to outcome 5:

"Consumers are provided with products that perform as firms

have led them to expect, and the associated service is of an acceptable standard and as they have been led to expect."

As per Chapter 2 of BCOBS, all information provided to customers post sale must be fair, clear and not misleading.'

In this document, the industry has accepted the need to provide customers with proper advice and help.

What is interesting is what this document leaves out. It does not require the banks to conduct a fair, efficient, thorough and speedy investigation. It might be argued that a bank has failed to 'act promptly, fairly and efficiently' where employees have responded in an aggressive and unhelpful manner to a complaint relating to unauthorised transactions, and where the bank does not investigate a complaint, or does not investigate the complaint with any due diligence. Some of the factors that should be considered in deciding whether the bank has acted with diligence will include, but not be limited to:

(i) How swiftly the bank put a stop on all future transactions after being informed by the customer that they were not responsible for a number of transactions.

(ii) The speed at which the bank physically inspected any ATM or point of sale terminal.

(iii) The quality of the technical evidence, and whether the bank made any attempt to balance the technical evidence from their logs relating to the transactions in dispute against the transaction counter on the customer's card.

(iv) Whether the bank took any steps to secure any relevant cctv recordings.

The position on the security systems used by the banks when operating ATMs and on-line banking is considered by section 5.9 of the *Industry Guidance for FSA Banking Conduct of Business Sourcebook*, as agreed by the banks themselves:

'5.9 Account security

To provide a fair and efficient service firms must provide secure and reliable banking systems. Important aspects of this process include having effective systems in place to allow customers to report thefts or losses and making available to customers useful information to help them protect their accounts. Such information could include:

- how to notify the firm promptly of any changes to the customer's personal information e.g. name, address and contact details;
- the benefits of checking statements and passbooks regularly and alerting the firm to any irregularities;
- how to keep cards, PINs, chequebooks, statements and security details safe; and
- how to alert the firm promptly to the loss of theft of any account details.

If using online banking:

- how to keep the customer's PC secure;
- how to keep passwords and PINS secret;
- the need to treat e-mails from senders claiming to be from the firm with caution and being wary of e-mails or calls asking for personal security details; and
- advising customers how to access internet banking sites by typing the bank or building society's address into the web browser i.e. not using a link in an e-mail.

Firms are encouraged to refer to the relevant rules at BCOBS 5.1.11 and 5.1.12 for details of a firm's and a customer's liabilities for unauthorised payments.'

The banks have accepted that they must 'provide secure and reliable banking systems.' Furthermore, the banks also accept that an important part of the process includes 'having effective systems in place to allow customers to report thefts or losses', but not, it seems, a fair, efficient, thorough and speedy investigation.

Chip and PIN technology has had an adverse effect on customers in two significant ways:

(i) When a correct PIN is entered, the bank assumes it is dealing with the customer, or a person authorised by the customer.

(ii) The systems used do not provide for different security mechanisms or settings for different types of use. This means a thief can obtain a PIN by observing a low-level transaction, and can then use the PIN for a high-level transaction.

Part of the problem for the banks, and by implication for those customers that are affected by unauthorised transactions, relates to the assumptions noted in (i) above. This is highlighted by a comment in the report 'Checking out chip and PIN: The Northampton trial report 2003' (Chip and PIN Programme Management Organisation), in which the authors provide a list of questions and answers, one of which is as follows (on page 21):

'What is a PIN?
A PIN (Personal Identification Number) is your 4-digit number which proves you are who you say you are. You tap in your PIN to verify a payment.'

This statement indicates a misunderstanding of what a PIN is and what it purports to do. The statement 'A PIN (Personal Identification Number) is your 4-digit number which proves you are who you say you are' is not correct. If this assertion was correct, then the fact that a transaction was carried out using the correct PIN would automatically mean it was the person to whom the card was issued who typed the PIN into a key pad. But a PIN is forged when it is keyed in by an unauthorised person, so the forgery obviously does not prove that the person who typed in the correct PIN is the person to whom the card was issued. The banks require customers to use a PIN in the full knowledge that when a PIN is forged, the issuer cannot tell the forged PIN from a PIN keyed in to an ATM by the customer. That the banks have chosen to use such a flimsy method of ascertaining their customers' agreement to a transaction with an ATM is their problem, and not the customer's – at least that is the legal position. But as any person who has had money removed from their account by a thief will be aware, making the bank understand that it was not the customer who withdrew the money can be far from easy.

A PIN on its own is not capable of proving you are who you say you are – in fact, a PIN even with some other form of link with your name (such as a credit card) is not capable of proving who you say you are. Both PINs and cards can be stolen and used by thieves without any fault on the part of their proper user.

Arguably, the PIN combines two functions. Before considering the two functions, consider the requirements of the bank. The bank needs to satisfy itself that the card is legitimate, and the card is in the possession of the customer to whom it was issued, or a person authorised by the customer to use the card. For the bank to be satisfied of these two facts, a series of communications takes place for ATM transactions. In short, the chip or magnetic stripe on the card is interrogated by the ATM and back end systems, a method of verification takes place between the card and the system with the PIN, and the card is duly authenticated to the satisfaction of the bank.

The first function of a PIN is to act as a means of authentication. In this respect, all a PIN might demonstrate is that *the person that keyed in the PIN knows the correct PIN*. However, if the attack described by Steven J. Murdoch, Saar Drimer, Ross Anderson and Mike Bond in their article 'Chip and PIN is Broken' in *31st IEEE Symposium on Security and Privacy*, (IEEE Computer Society, 2010) pp 433 – 446 is used by the thief, then any PIN can be used, and the banking systems will register the PIN as being correct.

Once the computer systems of the card issuer are satisfied that the card is legitimate and the PIN is the correct PIN of the card holder, then the second function of a PIN enables the person at the ATM to undertake any activity on the account that is permitted within the mandate and within the limitations of the technology.

It must be right to say that the PIN, even though it is offered to the machine before a transaction is effected, acts as a signature to verify the customer's authority to make a payment or other form of transaction. In this respect, the presentation of a card to an ATM, and the input of a PIN can be likened to a cheque that is written out by the account holder, signed, and then presented to the cashier at the bank. The customer completes the action necessary to request a payment in advance of the payment being made by the cashier, and then signs the cheque in the presence of the cashier – all before receiving acknowledgement that a transaction has been authorised. In this respect, the PIN is a form of electronic signature.

It is certain that a bank ought to have the duty to provide 'secure and reliable banking systems'.

Concluding remarks

Banking systems that are wholly run by using technology are not perfect. Such systems will always be subject to being successfully undermined by thieves. However, the imperfections of the technology do not provide a reason for customers to ignore the guidance issued by the authorities responsible for banking, or to fail to adhere to the contractual terms and conditions imposed by the banks. But even where a customer observes the guidance in full, it cannot be guaranteed that unauthorised transactions will not occur, especially as the result of the intervention of an intervening criminal act. In this respect, the provision of secure and reliable banking systems must be the cornerstone of any duty that a bank owes its customer, whether such duties are governed by negligence or a combination of contract and statute.

The only reason the weaknesses have been revealed in some instances, as discussed in this article, is because the banks were required to cooperate with the investigating authorities and explain and provide evidence of such weaknesses before the criminal courts. In civil actions, the banks have no incentive to reveal such weaknesses. The banks will deny that their systems suffer from any weaknesses, placing the blame squarely on the customer. It will be for the customer, should they ever have to consider taking legal action to recover money because of alleged unauthorised transactions that the bank will not reimburse, to point out to a judge that there is a series of cases that illustrate past weaknesses (some of which have yet to be remedied) that provide a good reason as to why the bank should be ordered to reveal, by way of example, any security evaluation performed on the bank's electronic banking system whether by its internal or external auditors, insurance inspectors, consultants or others supporting the claims of the bank that their system does not suffer from any weaknesses.

Unfortunately, not all banks respond well with complaints by customers, and if a matter gets as far as litigation, the banks tend to take an aggressive position in relation to the request by the customer, if such a request is ever made, for evidence that the bank has indeed put in place secure and reliable banking systems. It is for this reason that judges ought to take a robust view in favour of the customer. Even though the value of transactions that are the subject of theft that are acknowledged collectively by the banking sector is a tiny proportion of the value of the entire annual figure, nevertheless customers continue to suffer losses that they ascribe to the fault of the bank. It will be true to say that not every customer is right in their claim, but there are many instances where the bank uses its strength to ignore the failure of the security of its systems.

© Stephen Mason, 2012

Appendix 11

Electronic banking and how courts approach the evidence

by Stephen Mason

This article was published in the Computer Law and Security Review, Volume 29 Issue 2 (April 2013), 144 – 251

Key Points:

a) When a customer disputes a transaction or series of transactions that have taken place via an ATM and PIN, the evidence produced by the bank to prove its case is rarely adequate.

b) However, when a customer seeks to challenge the bank by way of informal adjudication methods or litigation, often the adjudicator or judge fails to understand the nature of the evidence required by the bank to prove its case.

c) Adjudicators and judges often accept assertions by banks about their security and the evidence generally without proving their claim.

Abstract:

Banking systems are so complex, that it is essential for a court to fully understand the weaknesses to be able to assess the evidence when faced with dealing with disputed transactions involving ATMs and on-line banking. A bank will make every effort to restrict the amount of evidence it has to provide to prove its case, but it is for the judge to be aware of the characteristics of electronic evidence, so that a fair trial can be conducted. This article considers the burden of proof in banking cases, and argues that not every court has succeeded in providing a claimant with a fair trial of the evidence.

This article compares the approaches taken by judges in dealing with disputes: disputes in which the customer claims that money has been withdrawn from their account without their permission or authority by way of the use of a combination of a card and an ATM or point-of-sale (POS) device. A customer might discover the unauthorised transactions took place even though their card never left their possession, and did not use it, or after their card was lost or stolen. It is suggested that some judges and Supreme Courts in some jurisdictions have, arguably, reached incorrect decisions based on a misunderstanding of the burden of proof, a failure to properly test the evidence, and an acceptance of unwarranted assumptions.

In circumstances where the bank refuses to reimburse the customer for the loss claimed, the bank invariably claims that the customer was grossly negligent, by asserting that either the PIN was written on the card; or that when the card was stolen with other items, the PIN was recorded on one of the other items in such a way that the PIN was obvious to the thief. This tends to be a statement made by the bank that purports to prove a fact, but has no basis in actuality, and there is no evidence to support the claim.

Since banks introduced information technology to provide services to customers, the most significant problem faced by banks is where a third party intervenes by undermining the technology between the bank and the customer for the purposes of theft. By way of example, one method is to take advantage of weaknesses in the technology, such as adding a small device inside the casing of the POS device used in garages and restaurants, so that when a card is inserted or swiped, the data is automatically transferred to thieves in another country.

Approaches by the courts

This article will consider a common claim: where the customer is adamant that they were neither responsible for, nor authorised the transactions in dispute. There are three aspects that are important that in turn illustrate that some judges and lawyers have struggled with the concept of electronic evidence and continue to do so:

(i) The burden of proof.

(ii) Attitudes to the evidence: that is, the nature of the evidence of the customer, and the assertions (usually without evidence) made by the bank.

(iii) The disclosure or discovery of relevant documents, or more accurately, the difficulty (or failure) to get appropriate disclosure.

The discussion that follows compares a number of relatively early cases to illustrate the issues.

The burden of proof

It is a familiar tenet of evidence that he who asserts must prove. In disputes involving banking, the bank must prove that it acted within the terms of the mandate. That is, where it relies on the signature of the customer, the bank must prove the transaction was authenticated by the customer's signature.[1] In terms of bank debit cards and ATMs, the PIN is the electronic signature of the customer. Within the European Union, a Directive now provides for the burden of proof in banking matters.[2] In the United Kingdom, the Directive has been enacted via the Payment Services Regulations 2009.[3] Regulation 60 sets out what the bank is required to prove:

> Evidence on authentication and execution of payment transactions
>
> 60.—(1) Where a payment service user—
>
> > (a) denies having authorised an executed payment transaction; or
> >
> > (b) claims that a payment transaction has not been correctly executed,
>
> it is for the payment service provider to prove that the payment transaction was authenticated, accurately recorded, entered in the payment service provider's accounts and not affected by a technical breakdown or some other deficiency.
>
> (2) In paragraph (1) "authenticated" means the use of any procedure by which a payment service provider is able to verify the use of a specific payment instrument, including its personalised security features.
>
> (3) Where a payment service user denies having authorised an executed payment transaction, the use of a payment instrument recorded by the payment service provider is not in itself necessarily sufficient to prove either that—
>
> > (a) the payment transaction was authorised by the payer; or
> >
> > (b) the payer acted fraudulently or failed with intent or gross negligence to comply with regulation 57.

A 'payment service provider' includes banks and issuers of credit. A 'payment service user' means a natural or legal person making use of a payment service, and a 'payment service' means using a debit card or credit card or on-line bank account.

This means the bank must produce evidence that:

> (i) The payment transaction was authenticated. This in turn means that the bank must demonstrate that the following procedures worked properly:
>
>> (a) the methods it uses to verify the use of the debit card and ATM or on-line banking account, and
>>
>> (b) how all of the personalised security features (e.g. PIN, password) worked.
>
> (ii) It was accurately recorded.
>
> (iii) It was entered in the payment service provider's accounts.
>
> (iv) It was not affected by a technical breakdown or some other deficiency.[4]

The bank must prove that the payment transaction was authorised by the payer. To do so, the bank must produce evidence to show that the customer's card was inserted into the ATM (or POS), that the customer's PIN was keyed in, and that the customer, or a person authorised by the customer, was responsible for carrying out the transaction. Often a bank will attempt to prove these two items with the flimsiest of evidence: normally by providing a few numbers and letters on a piece of paper, purporting to be data that supports the bank's case. What little evidence the bank produces, taken together, sets out the bank's chain of logic: if the software reports that the customer's card was inserted into the ATM and the customer's PIN was keyed in, then it follows that the customer's card was used and the correct PIN was keyed into the machine. Taking this logic one stage further, the bank then assumes that the customer was physically at the ATM, or somebody authorised by them. Where the customer claims they were not responsible for the transactions in dispute, the bank tends to claim that the customer was grossly negligent, in that not only did they allow a thief to get hold of the card, but they also recorded the PIN in such a way that the thief took possession of both the card and PIN. The underlying premise is that the technology is not only perfect, but it cannot be undermined in any way.

If the bank proves its case to the satisfaction of the court, it is then generally for the customer to raise sufficient evidence to make it probable that some other issue intervened: that is, a thief took advantage of the weaknesses in the IT systems of the bank to withdraw the money. This is far more difficult that it appears. In Germany and Austria, once the bank has got over the hurdle of proving the customer was the person responsible for the transaction, the burden shifts significantly, because the legal system employs the concept of the *prima facie* assumption. For instance, in an ATM case, the court then considers that the customer either:

> (i) violated their duty to keep the PIN secret by noting the PIN on the card; or
>
> (ii) breached their obligation to keep the PIN secret.

It is then for the customer to raise sufficient evidence to invalidate the evidence of the bank.

The concept of the prima facie assumption

The German case of 5 October 2004 before the Bundesgerichtshof (Federal Court of Justice)[5] illustrates the nature of the burden of proof and the concept of *prima facie* evidence. The facts were as follows: Between 3pm and 5pm on 23 September 2000, the plaintiff's purse was stolen during a city festival. It contained her eurocheque card (a cash card 'ec-card'). The ec-card was successfully used at the ATMs of two other banks by entering, it was alleged, the correct PIN. Two amounts of 500 DM were withdrawn on two separate occasions, and in the morning of the following day, the sum of 1,000 DM was also withdrawn. The plaintiff informed her bank of the loss of her card on 25 September 2000. The bank debited the plaintiff's current account with the amounts withdrawn from the ATMs.

The plaintiff claimed that the PIN was not written down, although it was saved in the form of a telephone number on her mobile telephone. The mobile telephone was not stolen. The Amtsgericht (District Court) decided in favour of the plaintiff's claim of reimbursement of the amount of 2,000 DM plus interest. On appeal, the Landgericht (Regional Court) rejected the plaintiff's claim. The plaintiff subsequently appealed to the Bundesgerichtshof to reinstate the judgment of the Amtsgericht.

The Bundesgerichtshof, in relying on the findings of fact by the Landgericht, upheld the view that in cases of the misuse of ec-cards and credit cards, the banks can rely on a *prima facie* presumption. The members of the court held that if a withdrawal is made from an ATM using the stolen card and the correct PIN shortly after the theft, a *prima facie* presumption applies that the customer noted the PIN on the card or stored the PIN with the card. The Bundesgerichtshof case law permits the application of a *prima facie* presumption where a fact to be proven is typical in the normal course of events, taking into account all the facts of the case. If causation is established and receives the benefit of a *prima facie* presumption, the other party can challenge the presumption on the basis of facts that cast serious doubt on whether the facts were typical.

In this instance, the bank adduced evidence from an authorised expert[6] that claimed that it was mathematically impossible to generate the PIN of an individual card as a result of the information present on the card without knowing the bank's cryptographic key. It was claimed that even with a significant financial effort, it would be impossible to design a computer that allows the calculation of the bank's cryptographic key.[7] The report went on to dismiss the possibility that a corrupt employee could have been responsible for the withdrawals, and that there was no evidence that the plaintiff's PIN was obtained by a third party.

Based on this evidence, the Landgericht concluded that the plaintiff was grossly negligent, and the *prima facie* evidence demonstrated that the plaintiff breached her duty of keeping the PIN secret, either by recording her PIN on the card or by storing it together with the card. The Bundesgerichtshof agreed with this conclusion, which means that both courts concluded that the theoretical possibilities put forward to explain the theft could not be considered seriously, noting that:

> 'In particular it has to be taken into consideration that the plaintiff *may have* noted the personal identification number on the ec-card or that the plaintiff *may have* stored this number together with the ec-card.' (emphasis added)

The members of the Bundesgerichtshof made an extraordinary statement in relation to the nature of the evidence:

> 'The District[9] Court has rightly come to the conclusion that the withdrawal with the original ec-card and the correct PIN by an unauthorised third party cannot be explained other than with the grossly negligent behaviour of the plaintiff. Other reasons might be possible in theory but after an evaluation they have to be considered as beyond the experience of life.'[10]

In essence, the decision was based on establishing that the plaintiff was a lair and that the banking systems were, ostensibly, perfect, which is demonstrably not true. In addition, there was no attempt to explain what the 'experience of life' meant, or the basis upon which the plaintiff could adduce evidence to the contrary. The case was decided on the basis that whatever evidence the bank adduced was accepted, and the plaintiff's claim that the thief must have decrypted the PIN or must have taken advantage of a deficiency in the bank's security system was rejected. This decision was criticised in Germany, and Dr Kritter pointed out a serious defect:

> 'The judgement was criticised in particular from consumer organisations. It was argued that the lower court had relied on an insufficient expert opinion, which to a great extent was based on assumptions as the bank had failed to provide the court's expert with sufficient facts as to the structure of PIN authentication system.'[11]

In essence, the court held that because it appeared to be impossible for a thief to decipher a PIN, then it must be the case that when a customer insists that they did not record the PIN – and does so consistently against all forms of cross-examination – it follows that they must be lying. With the greatest possible respect to the members of the court, this is not the correct approach to take. If the evidence of the plaintiff is clear, then it must be for the bank to demonstrate how robust its systems are. The fact is, that when banks are required to produce sufficient and compelling evidence to prove their case, they are often incapable of so doing – or unwilling to. There are now a significant number of well-documented methods by which thieves can take advantage of the weaknesses in the banks' technical systems.[12] In this respect, there are two observations to be noted:

> (i) Thieves are ahead of the game (if it can be considered a game), and the weaknesses they exploit now will not be known for some time – perhaps for years – or might not even be acted upon when uncovered.[13]

(ii) The usual response from the banks tends to follow a similar pattern when weaknesses are exposed, in that a spokesman or spokeswoman will make a statement to the effect that 'this is a theoretical attack, but not one that can be exploited in reality'.

In Norway, in a similar case in which a thief stole a number of cards, and where the customer claimed the PIN was not written down on or near the card, the court of first instance accepted the evidence provided by the bank,[14] and found against the plaintiff. It does not appear that the decision in this case was appealed. Of significance were some of the comments made by Assistant Judge Leif O. Østerbø who tried the case, in particular in relation to evidence that was never submitted to the court:[15]

> 'It is assumed that the standard security systems that are used are effective. However, according to Jørgensen, no cases have been documented that demonstrate the implementation of the systems are secure.
>
> The court refers in this respect to the fact that banks are subject to supervision and operate a comprehensive internal control work, and the witness Haugstad's explanation that both the standards and the practical implementation are revised thoroughly and regularly. In that regard, Haugestad explained that the systems are subject to annual audits. The Banks Control Center (BSK), in addition to the major international card companies, conducts such audits.
>
> The court does not find that there is reason to accept that the banks' security systems are in doubt. Although the implementation of a system necessarily involves opportunities for errors, the court cannot see that this involves significant practical risk for customers with cards.'

Given that the purpose of a trial is to test the evidence before the adjudicator reaches a decision, it is astounding that a judge would *assume* that the standard security systems used by the bank were effective; and accepted *untested* assurances that audits actually take place – not knowing whether such audits are conducted internally or by the Banks Control Center – not knowing whether the audits revealed problems that might affect the systems for ATMs and PINs – not knowing whether the audits were conducted by people with appropriate qualifications – leading to the conclusion that there was no reason to doubt the bank's security systems could be at fault.[16] The case of Pål-Gunnar Øiestad demonstrates the failure of a trial court to ensure all the appropriate evidence relied upon by the bank is not only submitted, also properly tested.[17] Pål-Gunnar Øiestad's credit card was stolen in 2008 in Rome, and over Nok 50,000 taken. The PIN was not written down, because it had been committed to memory. The bank claimed, without any evidence, that he was grossly negligent by keeping the PIN with the card. The Norwegian Complaints Board and the District Court agreed with the bank. Mr Øiestad was labelled a liar. While waiting for the appeal hearing, the bank wrote to him in June 2012, admitting it was wrong, which implies that the evidence submitted by the bank at trial was far from sufficient.[18]

As these cases illustrate, the question that lawyers must ask is: should judges be listening and acting on such unfounded assertions?

The correct approach

In comparison to the decision by the Bundesgerichtshof in 2004, the decision by the Lietuvos Aukšciausiasis Teismas (Supreme Court of Lithuania) in the case of *ŽŠ v Lietuvos taupomasis bankas*[19] is a textbook example of getting it right by a Supreme Court. In this case, ŽŠ deposited 800 Litas in cash into the bank account connected to his payment card on 26 August 1999, and deposited a further 48,200 Litas to the same account on 27 August 1999. On 29 August 1999, almost all the money had been withdrawn from the account by way of various ATM machines in Poland. ŽŠ claimed that he had not withdrawn the money. The bank refused to restore the sums of money that had been withdrawn.

The Vilnius 2nd district court dismissed the claim on 26 March 2001, on the basis that the bank was not at fault, nor was there a lack of care or diligence on the part of the bank's employees or contractors. On 13 June 2001, the members of the civil division of Vilnius Regional Court annulled the decision of Vilnius 2nd district court and awarded ŽŠ 48,423.52 Litas in damages. The panel of judges found that at the time the money was withdrawn from the ATM of the Gdansk bank in Bialystok city, Poland, the payment card issued by the bank was also used by ŽŠ in Lithuania. The bank did not refute the facts. The court concluded that the bank permitted the account to be debited using a payment card other than the one issued to ŽŠ, the bank having failed to establish that the money had been withdrawn by using the card and PIN issued to ŽŠ.

The members of the Supreme Court concluded that the evidence upon which the parties based their claims and rebuttals was insufficient, and the courts should have explained to each party their right to submit additional evidence, as well as the consequences of failing to provide the evidence required. In this instance, the members of the court concluded that the case was decided in violation of the rules on evidence and on the distribution of the burden of proof, which meant the case could have been decided incorrectly. As a result, the decisions of both were annulled, and the case had to be tried again.

The approach taken by the Supreme Court of Lithuania

The Supreme Court made the following observations, outlining the duties and liabilities of the bank (internal references omitted, taken almost verbatim from the translation, with permission of the publisher):

> (i) The business activity of banks is based upon the principles of stability, credibility, efficiency and safety. These principles form high standards of care and diligence for the banking business activity as a specific type of professional activity. A bank, being a specialised financial institution, has an obligation to act carefully and diligently in its professional activity, and this obligation also covers the bank's obligation to guarantee the credibility, efficiency and safety of its business. Assuming the attendant risks and responsibility means that the bank bears the burden of possible damages (losses) arising out of its business activity due to its insufficient credibility, efficiency and safety. Therefore, the bank's civil liability may arise because the bank violates a general obligation to ensure sufficient credibility, efficiency and safety of its activity in order to eliminate the possibility of damages (losses).[20]
>
> (ii) The taking of deposits and other repayable funds into clients' accounts and management of these accounts, the issuing of instruments of payment (cheques, letters of credit, bills, etc.) and the carrying out of transactions with them are professional activities of banks. Issuing and carrying out transactions with bank payment cards as an electronic payment instruments falls within the scope of definition of the banks' professional activity. The bank, which issues payment cards and carries out transactions with them, is obliged to ensure the credible, effective and safe functioning of its payment card system. By operating and administrating insufficiently safe systems, which do not ensure protection of payment cards from

fraud, systems that do not ensure protection of data required for the formation of payment orders, and systems that do not determine the personality of the person performing payments, the bank assumes the risks arising of operation of such systems.[21]

(iii) The bank must ensure the protection of payment cards against fraud. The bank bears the risk that the payment will be made with a fraudulent card or a substitute of the original card.[22]

Respecting the risk, the members of the court set out three items of relevance:[23]

(i) The bank bears the risk of damages (losses), related to the bank's activities of issuing payment cards into circulation and carrying out transactions with them.

(ii) The assumption of risk presupposes the bank's obligation to ensure the reliability, efficiency and security of the bank's payment cards system and an obligation to be alert while carrying out operations with payment cards. It forms the basis for the bank's liability not only for the lack of security of the payment cards themselves, but also for the lack of reliability and security of the bank's payment card system, and for establishing insufficiently reliable and secure necessary payment properties, and for the control of use of measures ensuring the reliability and security of the bank's payment card system, and for the security of the measures implemented by the bank.

(iii) The burden of proof in civil procedures is distributed, taking into consideration the general presumption of good faith of both parties, and evaluating which party is in a better position to prove its claims. The bank administrates and controls the payment card system and is responsible for the security of this system; the bank is obliged to act prudently and carefully. In comparison, bank's customers are not capable of affecting or influencing the reliability and security of the bank's payment card system. In administrating and controlling the system of settlement by payment cards, and implementing the security measures, the bank has a greater opportunity to prove that the security measures of the payment card are breached and all the necessary properties of the payment order are used due to the customer's fault; whereas the card holder has a lesser opportunity to prove the lack of fault on his part. It is for the bank to prove the specific actions of the card holder that caused the security measures to be neutralised with the customer's knowledge or due to the customer's lack of care or diligence. The burden of proof that the payment card security measures were breached only shifts to the card holder where it is established that the security measures could only be neutralised with the card holder's knowledge or because of the card holder's negligence.

In respect of the nature of the evidence submitted by the bank to prove its case, the members of the Supreme Court indicated that neither the court of first instance nor the appellate court checked whether the evidence submitted by the bank proved the claims that the original PIN was used and that it was entered correctly on the first attempt. The security level of the PIN had not been evaluated, notwithstanding the fact that evaluation of this level was of material significance to the determination of the evidentiary value of the use of the PIN in determining the correct distribution of the burden of proof between the parties to the dispute. There followed a list of 16 further items of evidence that the bank failed to submit to prove its case – much of which is obvious and ought to be included by a bank as a matter of course.[24]

Modern banking cases and the burden of proof

The cases referred to in this article are used merely to illustrate the nature of the evidence that has been adduced in trials relating to banking disputes, and does not represent the majority of decisions. With exceptions, it seems that the courts often accept what is tantamount to the worst superficial evidence from banks to prove 'facts'. The banks have been successful in making a range of unsubstantiated assertions, such as comments relating to the 'security of the system' (whatever that means) and the 'impossibility of cracking the encryption' (in the absence of the relevance of this issue), and they do so by the use of witnesses that are permitted to give their opinions based on erroneous assumptions about their assurances that there is no proof that their systems have been successfully undermined by thieves.

Courts have made mistakes by refraining from ensuring that the nature and quality of the evidence is properly tested. In addition to which, courts make erroneous assumptions about the evidence before them that is not warranted, as in the case of Bernt Petter Jørgensen. In this light, Stanley Burnton LJ made some comments in *O'Shea v R* in passing, that 'It is also surprising in the extreme that if the supposed fraudulent webmaster was able to debit the appellant's credit card account, he did so for such limited amounts and on relatively few occasions. This, is however, a minor point.'[25] With the deepest possible respect to Stanley Burnton LJ, this observation is not totally accurate. The evidence demonstrates that although thieves will attempt (and have succeeded) to steal large sums of money, nevertheless, there is a tendency to steal a small sum (sometimes of just US$10 and often less) from hundreds of thousands of accounts, rather than a large sum from a single account – thus producing more success, because it takes longer for the ruse to be discovered by customers and banks. Unfortunately, if judges continue to make judgments based on assumptions, rather than facts, then all will remain unwell in banking disputes.

Lawyers must be actively aware of the lack of evidence in banking disputes. It is essential for a lawyer representing a customer of a bank that they must demand to see the relevant evidence the bank relies upon to prove its case. The lawyer must be attentive where there is insufficient evidence; of the failure to prove relevant evidence, and to challenge the assumptions made by bank witnesses, as well as the assumptions made by judges, and to challenge the presumption that a computer is 'reliable' or 'working properly'. The prevalence of errors in code is such that it is dangerous to apply to computers the general assumption that machines do not lie, however appropriate this may once have been to simple cash registers.[26] In essence, the lawyer must have a good command of the technical issues, as well as to understand and challenge the vague assumptions that are made about the way thieves operate.

This is especially relevant in the light of the underlying rationale of *A Philosophy of Evidence Law Justice in the Search for Truth*[27] by Professor Hock Lai Ho, in which he demonstrates that the finder of fact acts as a moral agent, and central to this is that the findings by a court must be justifiable, and meet the demands of rationality and ethics. In this text, Professor Ho analyses the debate on the claim that the trial process seeks the truth, exploring the connection between truth and justice.[28] When read in the light of the unique characteristics of digital evidence, the text, stimulating and interesting as it is, takes on an even more relevant role – a role that the author might not have contemplated. This is because the factors and subsequent analysis have an added poignancy when taking into account the complexity of digital evidence; the potential volumes of evidence; the difficulty of finding evidence; persuading the judge to order additional searches or to order the disclosure of evidence; the ease by which digital evidence can be destroyed; the costs of such exercises and the lawyer's lack of knowledge when dealing with this form of evidence. In this respect, the inadequacy of the procedure leading to trial may cause unfairness, as Professor Ho demonstrates:[29]

> 'Verdicts might well be shown to be false by evidence which was not brought before the court. This possibility led Lord Wilberforce to hold in *Air Canada & Ors v Secretary of State for Trade* ([1983] 2 AC 394, at 438) that so long as the court makes its findings 'in accordance with the available evidence and the law, justice will have been fairly done.' We can demand from the court the fair dispensation of justice; but we misunderstand the purpose and nature of the trial if we expect it to produce the objective truth. On this view, truth is not essential for justice. Or, as Viscount Kilmuir puts it, 'justice comes before truth.' ((1960) 76 LQR 41, 43).
>
> Lord Wilberforce and Viscount Kilmuir seem to equate justice with fair process. This is a construal of justice that judges, conscious of the fallibility of legal fact-finding, and anxious not to attract undue criticisms, are especially keen to spread. Lord Devlin joined the two judges in spreading the message:
>
>> Provided that he had been given a fair trial and that the judge has been seen to be careful and impartial, a plaintiff who has been wrongly disbelieved, painful though it may be, ought not to feel that he has been the victim of injustice.
>>
>> But surely the plaintiff (and, all the more so, a defendant who has been convicted of a crime she did not commit) has every right to feel aggrieved.'

Professor Ho suggests that the parties may be rightly aggrieved if concerns of procedure and costs override the search for truth – rightly, it is suggested. Of increasing concern in modern cases is the cost of finding and submitting digital evidence – and in addition, the resistance, especially of banks, to submit proper evidence to support their assertions, in particular with respect to unauthorised withdrawals from ATMs and on-line banking disputes. The consequences that inevitably flow from a decision means that it is linked to claims of morality, and a judgment cannot be supported where it is reached in a cavalier manner.

This argument is, in turn, affected by the 'overriding objective' of the Civil Procedure Rules in England and Wales. For instance, should the bank refuse to provide evidence that the customer claims is relevant, the customer must ask a judge for an order that the bank disclose evidence. In such circumstances, the bank will invariably resist the granting of such an order, and it will pray in aid the 'overriding objective', which forms paragraph 1.1 of the Civil Procedure Rules. This reads as follows:

> (1) These Rules are a new procedural code with the overriding objective of enabling the court to deal with cases justly.
>
> (2) Dealing with a case justly includes, so far as is practicable –
> (a) ensuring that the parties are on an equal footing;
> (b) saving expense;
> (c) dealing with the case in ways which are proportionate –
> (i) to the amount of money involved;
> (ii) to the importance of the case;
> (iii) to the complexity of the issues; and
> (iv) to the financial position of each party;
> (d) ensuring that it is dealt with expeditiously and fairly; and
> (e) allotting to it an appropriate share of the court's resources, while taking into account the need to allot resources to other cases.

There are many aspects to the overriding objective, but the bank will invariably attempt to use items (2)(b) and (c)(i) in isolation to argue that any requests for additional documents will be contrary to the need to keep costs down. The bank will rarely address the most significant issue: the complexity of the case. It is for this reason that whenever additional documents are requested from the bank, it is essential for the judge to be alert to the intricate nature of modern banking systems, and that much of the technical evidence is required by both parties, otherwise neither party would know what the facts are; in addition to which, the bank would be in danger of failing to prove its case if it fails to produce relevant evidence. It is therefore incumbent on the judge to ensure that the legal system is not manipulated by the banking system to avoid liability, for as Professor Kaplow has indicated:

> '... decision criteria for adjudication – the setting of proof burdens in various legal contexts – should rest on a stronger foundation than age-old dicta. They should instead be grounded in explicit analysis that attends to the consequences of legal outcomes:

correct and mistaken imposition of liability as well as proper and erroneous exoneration.'[30]

Professor Kaplow goes on to comment that:

> 'Deterrence of wrongful conduct is central not only to controlling crime but also to inducing individuals to perform contracts, comply with environmental and health regulations, avoid careless activity, and interact honestly in the marketplace. The control of harmful behavior is, of course, the raison d'être for the legal system, and it is crucial to consider how the system's ability to achieve this objective is affected by how high the burden of proof is set.'

In the case of electronic banking, the effective imposition of the burden of proof by judges might act to cause banks to consider more carefully the avoidance of careless activities – for their computer systems are clearly deficient.[31]

There is also a problem with the notion of keeping costs proportionate. The danger is that in a banking dispute for a small amount of money, unless the judge is aware of the complicated nature of banking systems, they are less likely to order the bank to provide relevant critical information about the state of its IT systems, or to enable the customer to interrogate relevant members of staff, because the cost of so doing will far outweigh the amount in dispute.

However, in riposte to any such argument, article 6 of the European Convention for the Protection of Human Rights and Fundamental Freedoms is an enactment that can be used, and ought to be successful against any claim by the bank about the costs of providing the relevant evidence. The first sentence of article 6 provides:

> 'In the determination of his civil rights and obligations or of any criminal charge against him, everyone is entitled to a fair and public hearing within a reasonable time by an independent and impartial tribunal established by law.'

Parties have a right to a fair hearing, which must imply that there is a right to test the relevant evidence, no matter how difficult or expensive it is to obtain.

© Stephen Mason, 2012

1 For case law in relation to PINs, see Stephen Mason, *Electronic Signatures in Law* (3rd edn, Cambridge University Press, 2012); also on electronic signatures and technical regulations, see Lorna Brazell, *Electronic Signatures and Identities Law and Regulation* (2nd edn, Sweet & Maxwell, 2008).
2 Directive 2007/64/EC of the European Parliament and of the Council of 13 November 2007 on payment services in the internal market amending Directives 97/7/EC, 2002/65/EC, 2005/60/EC and 2006/48/EC and repealing Directive 97/5/EC (Text with EEA relevance) OJ L319, 5.12.2007, p. 1–36).
3 Statutory Instrument 2009 No. 209.
4 The requirement is similar to the test for authenticity proposed in Stephen Mason, general editor, *Electronic Evidence* (3rd edn, LexisNexis Butterworths, 2012), chapter 4.
5 XI ZR 210/03, published BGHZ 160, 308-321, translated into English in the *Digital Evidence and Electronic Signature Law Review* 6 (2009), 248 – 254, with commentaries by Dr Martin Eßer and Dr Thomas Kritter.
6 To give expert evidence in German courts, the expert is usually appointed from a list of publicly certified experts admitted at court (*öffentlich bestellte Sachverständige*), for which see Dr. Alexander Duisberg and Dr. Henriette Picot, 'Germany' in Stephen Mason, gen ed, *International Electronic Evidence* (British Institute of International and Comparative Law, 2008), 335.
7 Paragraph 15 of the judgment.
8 Paragraph 14.
9 There is a confusion in the translation as to whether the Landgericht is a Regional or District court. It appears that the Landgericht is a Regional Court, and so the words 'Regional Court' should appear in the translation, not District Court.
10 Paragraph 28(a).
11 *Digital Evidence and Electronic Signature Law Review* 6 (2009), 254.
12 A list is provided in Stephen Mason, *Electronic Banking: Protecting Your Rights* (PP Publishing, 2012), chapter 3.
13 Dr Saar Drimer and Dr Steven J. Murdoch at the University of Cambridge demonstrated in 2009 and in 2011 that a thief can use a small hand-held device, called Smart Card Detective, which intercepts the communication between the card and the terminal. This device allows the thief to key in any PIN, and the ATM or terminal will be fooled into accepting it was the correct PIN. The banks have not stopped this very dangerous weakness in 2012: Steven J. Murdoch, Saar Drimer, Ross Anderson and Mike Bond, 'Chip and PIN is Broken' in *31st IEEE Symposium on Security and Privacy*, (IEEE Computer Society, 2010) pp 433 – 446.
14 *Bernt Petter Jørgensen v DnB NOR Bank ASA*, Journal number 04-016794TVI-TRON, Trondheim District Court, 24 September 2004. For a translation into English, see *Digital Evidence and Electronic Signature Law Review* 9 (2012), 117 – 123.
15 Translation, 122.
16 For an indication of what can be wrong with the security system of a bank, see Ken Lindup, 'Technology and banking: Lessons from the past', *Digital Evidence and Electronic Signature Law Review* 9 (2012), 91 – 94.
17 Discussed in Maryke Silalahi Nuth, 'Unauthorized use of bank cards with or without the PIN: a lost case for the customer?', *Digital Evidence and Electronic Signature Law Review* 9 (2012), 95 – 101.
18 A translation into English of the letter sent to Mr Øiestad is set out in full as an annex to the article by Maryke Silalahi Nuth, 'Unauthorized use of bank cards with or without the PIN: a lost case for the customer?'.
19 No. 3K-3-390/2002; for a translation of the judgment into English by Sergejs Trofimovs, see *Digital Evidence and Electronic Signature Law Review* 6 (2009), 255 – 262.

20 Translation, 257 – 258.
21 Translation, 258.
22 Translation, 258.
23 Translation, 259.
24 To a certain extent, this line of argument occurred in a Turkish case, 2009/11485, judgment number 2011/4033 before the Supreme Court of Appeal, Civil Law Circuit on 7 April 2011 in a case involving unauthorised transfer of funds by a thief over the internet, for a translation of the judgment into English by Av. Burcu Orhan Holmgren, see *Digital Evidence and Electronic Signature Law Review* 9 (2012), 124 – 127.
25 *O'Shea v R* [2010] EWCA Crim 2879 at [56].
26 This was the subject of submissions in the case of *Job v Halifax PLC* (not reported) Case number 7BQ00307, the full judgment of which is published in *Digital Evidence and Electronic Signature Law Review* 6 (2009), 235 – 245; see Stephen Mason, general editor, *Electronic Evidence*, chapter 5 in relation to the 'reliability' of computers and the prevalence of errors in software.
27 Oxford University Press, 2008.
28 Note the recent article by Louis Kaplow, 'Burden of Proof', 121 Yale L.J. 738 (2012), in which the author considers how robust the evidence ought to be in order to assign liability when the objective is to maximize social welfare.
29 Hock Lai Ho, *A Philosophy of Evidence Law Justice in the Search for Truth*, 64 – 65.
30 Louis Kaplow, 'Burden of Proof', 745.
31 Stephen Mason, 'UK credit card fraud: the scale of the problem', *e-Finance & Payments Law & Policy*, January 2012, Volume 06, Issue 01, 14 – 16.

Appendix 12

Further information

A note about web site addresses: an address for a web site might change. The web site addresses given below are correct at the time this book was published.

Journal

Digital Evidence and Electronic Signature Law Review (free)
http://journals.sas.ac.uk/deeslr

Reporting theft

Guidance has been issued to the police and financial institutions, and is included in the Home Office Counting Rules for Recorded Crime (specifically 'Counting Rules for fraud and forgery'), these are public documents and they are available at:
https://www.gov.uk/government/uploads/system/uploads/attachment_data/file/177109/count-fraud-april-2013.pdf
Action Fraud: http://www.actionfraud.police.uk/

Submissions to Parliament

Stephen Mason and Nicholas Bohm, 'Banking and Fraud' a written submission to the Treasury Committee on 17 January 2011:
http://www.publications.parliament.uk/pa/cm201011/cmselect/cmtreasy/430/430vw25.htm

Courts

For forms: http://www.justice.gov.uk/forms/hmcts
Courts and Tribunals: http://www.justice.gov.uk/courts

The Civil Procedure Rules and Practice Directions:
http://www.justice.gov.uk/courts/procedure-rules/civil/rules

Her Majesty's Courts Service Money Claim Online:
https://www.moneyclaim.gov.uk/web/mcol/welcome

Information about making a claim

'Portal' web site to follow links for forms and leaflets:
http://hmctsformfinder.justice.gov.uk/HMCTS/FormFinder.do

Court leaflets and forms

How do I make a court claim? (EX302)
No reply to my claim form – What should I do? (EX304)
The fast track and the multi-track in civil courts (EX305)
The defendant disputes all or part of my claim (EX306)
The small claims track (EX307)
Court fees – Do I have to pay them? (EX160A)
N1 Claim form

Case law mentioned

The Guardians of Halifax Union v Wheelwright (1873-74) 9 – 10 L.R.Exch. 183

Legal practitioner textbooks

New editions of the books below are published each year. These are the practitioner textbooks used by lawyers in the courts. They are expensive, but might be available in some public libraries. If you have a problem with any aspect of civil procedure, should you decide to be a litigant in person, the texts in these books should help you formulate your arguments before a judge. This is particularly relevant if the bank will not provide you with the evidence and you have to ask a judge for an order that the bank provides you with the relevant evidence.
Civil Procedure (White Book) (Sweet & Maxwell)
The Civil Court Practice (The Green Book) (LexisNexis Butterworths)

Help and explanations provided about taking legal action

Citizen's Advice Bureau:
http://www.adviceguide.org.uk/

Disabled

HM Courts and Tribunals Service Disability Helpline: 0800 358 3506 between 9am and 5pm, Monday to Friday. If you are deaf or hard of hearing, you can use the Minicom service: 0191 478 1476

Mediation and alternative dispute resolution

Ministry of Justice, find a mediation service:
http://www.civilmediation.justice.gov.uk/

Advice Services Alliance, ADRnow: http://www.adrnow.org.uk/

Banking authorities

The Financial Markets Law Committee: **http://www.fmlc.org/**

LINK consumer Committee:
http://www.link.co.uk/Cardholders/Pages/ConsumerCommittee.aspx

Financial Ombudsman Service:
http://www.financial-ombudsman.org.uk/

The Financial Ombudsman Service produce a regular briefing called 'News'. A number of issues include case reports relating to bank cards and on-line banking.

Financial Ombudsman Service Limited Banking & Finance Case Studies
http://www.fos.org.au/centric/home_page/cases/banking_finance_case_studies.jsp

Financial Conduct Authority: **http://www.fca.org.uk/**

Prudential Regulation Authority:
http://www.bankofengland.co.uk/pra/Pages/default.aspx

Consumer Protection and Markets Authority (no web site at the time of publication)

Banking: Conduct of Business sourcebook (FSA)
http://www.fsa.gov.uk/doing/regulated/banking/bcobs

European Central Bank

European Central Bank, Report on card fraud (2012),
https://www.ecb.europa.eu/pub/pdf/other/cardfraudreport201207en.pdf

European Central Bank, Second Report on card fraud (July 2013,
https://www.ecb.europa.eu/pub/pdf/other/cardfraudreport201307en.pdf

European Central Bank, Recommendations for the security of internet payments (April 2012):
http://www.ecb.int/press/pr/date/2013/html/pr130131_1.en.html

Banking organisations

CIFAS: **http://www.cifas.org.uk/**

UK Payments Administration Limited (previously known as APACS):
http://www.ukpayments.org.uk/

'Industry Guidance for FSA Banking Conduct of Business Sourcebook' (British Bankers' Association, Building Societies Association, Payments Council, January 2011) http://www.bba.org.uk/media/article/industry-guidance-for-fsa-banking-conduct-of-business-sourcebook

The UK Cards Association: http://www.theukcardsassociation.org.uk/2011-facts-figures/index.asp

On-line web sites with advice about banking threats

Bank Safe Online: http://www.banksafeonline.org.uk/

Financial Fraud Action UK (previously Card Watch), has some information about card fraud figures and advice: http://www.financialfraudaction.org.uk/

Get Safe Online: http://www.getsafeonline.org/

Action Fraud: http://www.identitytheft.org.uk/

European ATM Security & Fraud Prevention: https://www.european-atm-security.eu/Welcome%20to%20EAST/

EU Fraud Prevention Expert Group http://ec.europa.eu/internal_market/fpeg/index_en.htm

ATMSecurity.com, a web site with news items run by DFR Risk Management: http://www.atmsecurity.com/

Chip and Pin: http://www.chipandpin.co.uk/

National Fraud Authority: https://www.gov.uk/government/organisations/national-fraud-authority/about

University of Cambridge Security Group Banking Security: http://www.cl.cam.ac.uk/research/security/banking/

The Financial Services Club's Blog: http://www.thefinanser.co.uk/

ATM Security.com: http://www.atmsecurity.com/monthly-digest/atm-security-monthly-digest/atm-fraud-and-security-digest-september-2009.html

The Bank Fraud Resource Page: http://www.cl.cam.ac.uk/~rja14/banksec.html

Other web sites of relevance

Office of Fair Trading: http://www.oft.gov.uk/

Electronic Funds Transfer Code of Conduct http://www.asic.gov.au/asic/asic.nsf/byheadline/Electronic+Funds+Transfer:+Code+of+Conduct?opendocument

European Union Agency for Network and Information Security

Professor Manel Medina, Dr Jetzabel Serna, Andreas Sfakianakis, Jordi Aguilá and Luis Ángel Fernández, eID Authentication methods in eFinance and e-Payment services Current practices and Recommendations (European Union Agency for Network and Information Security Report, December 2013): http://www.enisa.europa.eu/activities/identity-and-trust/library/deliverables/eIDA-in-e-finance-and-e-payment-services

Independent views on banking

Chip and Spin: **http://www.chipandspin.co.uk/**

Light Blue Touchpaper: **http://www.lightbluetouchpaper.org/**

Phantom Withdrawals: **http://www.phantomwithdrawals.com/index.php/Phantom_Withdrawals**

The Bank Fraud Resource Page, maintained by Professor Ross Anderson: **http://www.cl.cam.ac.uk/~rja14/banksec.html**

Bankers Online: **http://www.bankersonline.com/infovault/courtwatch.html**
Financial cryptography: **https://www.financialcryptography.com/**

Anti-virus

AV-Comparatives.org **http://www.av-comparatives.org/**

Academics

Professor Ross Anderson: **http://www.cl.cam.ac.uk/~rja14/**

Mike Bond: **http://www.cl.cam.ac.uk/~mkb23/**

Professor Chris Mitchell, Information Security Group, Royal Holloway,
University of London: **http://www.isg.rhul.ac.uk/**

Dr Steven J. Murdoch: **http://www.cl.cam.ac.uk/~sjm217/**

Dr Richard Clayton: **http://www.cl.cam.ac.uk/~rnc1/**

Dr Saar Drimer: **http://www.cl.cam.ac.uk/~sd410/**

Selected articles

Ben Adida, Mike Bond, Jolyon Clulow, Amerson Lin, Steven Murdoch, Ross Anderson, and Ron Rivest, Phish and Chips (Traditional and

New Recipes for Attacking EMV)
http://www.cl.cam.ac.uk/~rja14/Papers/Phish-and-Chips.pdf

Ross Anderson, 'Why Cryptosystems Fail'
http://www.cl.cam.ac.uk/~rja14/wcf.html

Nicholas Bohm and Stephen Mason, 'Identity and its verification' *Computer Law & Security Review*, Volume 26, Number 1, January 2010, 43 – 51

Mike Bond, Omar Choudary, Steven J. Murdoch, Sergei Skorobogatov and Ross Anderson, 'Chip and Skim: cloning EMV cards with the pre-play attack', a paper presented to Cryptographic Hardware and Embedded System (CHES) 2012, in Leuven, Belgium, September 2012, http://www.lightbluetouchpaper.org/2012/09/10/chip-and-skim-cloning-emv-cards-with-the-pre-play-attack/

Joseph Bonneau, Sören Preibusch and Ross Anderson, 'A birthday present every eleven wallets? The security of customer-chosen banking PINs' (Computer Laboratory, University of Cambridge, 2012) www.cl.cam.ac.uk/~jcb82/doc/BPA12-FC-banking_pin_security.pdf

David J. Boyd, 'Enhancing the Non-Repudiation Properties of the EMV Payment Cards'
http://www.albany.edu/iasymposium/proceedings/2008/16-BoydEdit.pdf

Adam R. Brentnall, Martin J. Crowder and David J. hand, 'A statistical model for the temporal pattern of individual automated teller machine withdrawals', *Applied Statistics Journal of the Royal Statistical Society*, Volume 57, Issue 1, February 2008, pp 43 – 59

Mohammed AlZomai, Bander Alfayyadh, Audun Jøsang and Adrian McCullagh, 'An experimental investigation of the usability of transaction authorization in online bank security systems', in Ljilana Brankovic and Mirka Miller, eds, *Proceedings of the sixth Australasian conference on Information security – Volume 81* (Australian Computer Society, Inc., 2008), pp 65-73, available at http://crpit.com/abstracts/CRPITV81AlZomai.html

Bander AlFayyadh, James Ponting, Mohamed Alzomai and Audun Jøsang, 'Vulnerabilities in Personal Firewalls Caused by Poor Security Usability' in 2010 IEEE International Conference on Information Theory and Information Security (ICITIS) Beijing, 17-19 December 2010, (IEEE, 2010) pp 682-688, available at
http://folk.uio.no/josang/papers/APAJ2010-ICITIS.pdf

Daniel Bilar, 'Known knowns, known unknowns and unknown unknowns: anti-virus issues, malicious software and internet attacks for non-technical audiences' *Digital Evidence and Electronic Signature Law Review*, 6 (2009) 123 – 131

Mike Bond and Piotr Zieliński, 'Decimalisation table attacks for PIN cracking' (Technical Report Number 560, February 2003, Computer Laboratory, University of Cambridge, UCAM-CL-TR-560) http://www.cl.cam.ac.uk/techreports/UCAM-CL-TR-560.pdf

Adam R. Brentnall, Martin J. Crowder and David J. hand, 'A statistical model for the temporal pattern of individual automated teller machine withdrawals', *Applied Statistics Journal of the Royal Statistical Society*, Volume 57, Issue 1, February 2008, pp 43 – 59

Liang Cai and Hao Chen, TouchLogger: Inferring Keystrokes On Touch Screen From Smartphone Motion, https://www.usenix.org/legacy/event/hotsec11/tech/final_files/Cai.pdf

Saar Drimer, Steven J. Murdoch and Ross Anderson, 'Thinking inside the box: system-level failures of tamper proofing' (Technical Report Number 711, Computer Laboratory, University of Cambridge, February 2008, UCAM-CL-TR-711) http://www.cl.cam.ac.uk/techreports/UCAM-CL-TR-711.pdf

C. Dufva, J. Bengtsson, M. Svensson and A. Nilsson, 'Forensic analysis of magnetic stripe skimmer devices', *Forensic Science International: Genetics Supplement Series*, Series 3 (2011) e385-e386 http://liu.academia.edu/Departments/Department_of_Science_and_Technology/Papers

Martin Georgiev, Subodh Iyengar, Suman Jana, Rishita Anubhai, Dan Boneh and Vitaly Shmatikov, The Most Dangerous Code in the World: Validating SSL Certificates in Non-Browser Software (19th *ACM Conference on Computer and Communications Security*, 16-18 October 2012), https://crypto.stanford.edu/~dabo/pubs/abstracts/ssl-client-bugs.html

Assistant Professor DDr Gerwin Haybäck, 'Civil law liability for unauthorized withdrawals at ATMs in Germany', *Digital Evidence and Electronic Signature Law Review*, 6 (2009) 57 – 66

Ken Lindup, 'Technology and banking: lessons from the past', *Digital Evidence and Electronic Signature Law Review*, 9 (2012) 91 – 94

Václav (Vashek) Matyáš, Jan Krhovják, Marek Kumpost and Daniel Cvrcek, 'Authorizing Card Payments with PINs' *Computer*, (Los Alamitos, IEEE Computer Society, USA), 2008, volume 41, number 2, pp 64 – 68

Stephen Mason, 'When the chips are down: The bank, the PIN & the ATM' *New Law Journal*, Volume 159, No 7376, 10 July 2009, p 976

Stephen Mason and Roger Porkess, 'Chip & pin fallacies' *New Law*

Journal, Volume 159, No 7389, 16 October 2009, pp 1413 – 1414

Stephen Mason, 'UK credit card fraud: the scale of the problem', *e-Finance & Payments Law & Policy,* January 2012, Volume 06, Issue 01, pp 14 – 16

Stephen Mason, 'Debit cards, ATMs and negligence of the bank and customer', *Butterworths Journal of International Banking and Financial Law,* Volume 27, Number 3, March 2012, 163 – 173

Stephen Mason, 'Electronic banking and how courts approach the evidence', *Computer Law and Security Review*, Volume 29, Issue 2 (April 2013), 144 – 151

Keaton Mowery, Sarah Meiklejohn and Stefan Savage, 'Heat of the Moment: Characterizing the Efficacy of Thermal Camera-Based Attacks'
http://www.usenix.org/events/woot11/tech/final_files/Mowery.pdf

Steven J. Murdoch, 'Reliability of Chip & PIN evidence in banking disputes', *Digital Evidence and Electronic Signature Law Review*, 6 (2009) 98 – 115

Steven J. Murdoch, Mike Bond and Ross Anderson, 'How Certification Systems Fail: Lessons from the Ware Report', *IEEE Security & Privacy*, Nov-Dec 2012, volume 10, issue 6, pp 40–44
http://www.cl.cam.ac.uk/~sjm217/papers/ieeesp12warereport.pdf

Maryke Silalahi Nuth, 'Unauthorized use of bank cards with or without the PIN: a lost case for the customer?', *Digital Evidence and Electronic Signature Law Review*, 9 (2012), 95 – 101

Roger Porkess and Stephen Mason, 'Looking at debit and credit card fraud', *Teaching Statistics*, Volume 34, Number 3, Autumn 2012, 87 – 91

Laurent Simon and Ross Anderson, PIN Skimmer: Inferring PINs Through The Camera and Microphone (University of Cambridge), http://www.cl.cam.ac.uk/~rja14/Papers/pinskimmer_spsm13.pdf

Graham Steel, 'Formal Analysis of PIN Block Attacks', *Theoretical Computer Science – Automated reasoning for security protocol analysis*, Volume 367 Issue 1, 24 November 2006, pp 257 – 270

Selected academic dissertations

Omar S. Choudary, *The Smart Card Detective: a hand-held EMV interceptor* (University of Cambridge, Computer Laboratory, Darwin College, June 2010, dissertation for the degree of Master of Philosophy in Advanced Computer Science)

http://www.cl.cam.ac.uk/~osc22/docs/mphil_acs_osc22.pdf

Gerhard de Koning Gans, Outsmarting Smart Cards, PhD dissertation, 2013, http://www.cs.ru.nl/~flaviog/theses/Outsmarting_Smart_Cards.pdf

Selected books

Ross J. Anderson, *Security Engineering: A Guide to Building Dependable Distributed Systems* (2nd edition, Wiley, 2008)

David Emmett, *Drafting* (Oxford University Press) – this text is published every year, so if you decide to obtain a copy, you need to find the most recent copy

Stephen Mason, *Electronic Signatures in Law* (3rd edn, Cambridge University Press, 2012)

Stephen Mason, general editor, *Electronic Evidence* (3rd edn, LexisNexis Butterworths, 2012)

Kevin D. Mitnick and William L. Simon, *The Art of Deception* (Wiley Publishing, Inc, 2002)

Bruce Schneier, *Secrets and Lies Digital Security in a Networked World* (Wiley Computer Publishing, 2000)

Selected chapters in books

Saar Drimer, Steven J. Murdoch and Ross Anderson, 'Optimised to Fail: Card Readers for Online Banking' in Roger Dingledine and Philippe Golle, editors, *Financial Cryptography and Data Security*, 13th International Conference, Lecture Notes in Computer Science Volume 5628 (Springer, 2009), pp 184 – 200
http://www.cl.cam.ac.uk/~sjm217/papers/fc09optimised.pdf

A. Theodore Markettos and Simon W. Moore, 'The Frequency Injection Attack on Ring-Oscillator-Based True Random Number Generators', in Christophe Clavier and Kris Gaj, editors, *Proceedings of the 11th International Workshop on Cryptographic Hardware and Embedded Systems* (Springer-Verlag Berlin, 2009), pp 317 – 331

Steven J. Murdoch, Saar Drimer, Ross Anderson and Mike Bond, 'Chip and PIN is Broken' in *31st IEEE Symposium on Security and Privacy*, (IEEE Computer Society, 2010) pp 433 – 446
http://www.cl.cam.ac.uk/~sjm217/papers/oakland10chipbroken.pdf

Steven J. Murdoch and Ross Anderson, 'Verified by Visa and MasterCard SecureCode: or, How Not to Design Authentication', in Radu Sion, editor, *Financial Cryptography and Data Security*, 14th International Conference, Lecture Notes in Computer Science,

Volume 6052 (Springer 2010), pp 336 – 342
http://www.cl.cam.ac.uk/~rja14/Papers/fc10vbvsecurecode.pdf

Jason F. Reid and Mark H. Looi, 'Making Sense of Smart Card Security Certifications', in Josep Domingo-Ferrer, David Chan and Anthony Watson, editors, *Proceedings of the fourth working conference on smart card research and advanced applications on Smart card research and advanced applications* (Kluwer Academic Publishers Norwell, MA, USA, 2001), pp 225 – 240
http://eprints.qut.edu.au/344/

Selected reports

ATM crime: Overview of the European situation and golden rules on how to avoid it (European Network and Information Security Agency, August 2009)
http://www.enisa.europa.eu/act/ar/deliverables/2009/atmcrime

Banking & Finance Policies and Procedures Manual (Extract dealing with Credit Card Disputes and Electronic Funds Transfer Investigations) (Financial Ombudsman Service, 2008)
http://www.fos.org.au/public/download.jsp?id=3306

Raymond J. Butler, *The Role of Spreadsheets in the Allied Irish Bank/Allfirst Currency Trading Fraud*, http://arxiv.org/pdf/0910.2048.pdf

Malicious Software (Malware): *A Security Threat to the Internet Economy*, (Ministerial Background Report DSTI/ICCP/REG(2007)5/FINAL, OECD Directorate for Science, Technology and Industry Committee for Information, Computer and Communications Policy)
http://www.oecd.org/dataoecd/53/34/40724457.pdf

Debbie Moon (ed), John Flatley (ed), Jacqueline Hoare, Bryony Green and Rachel Murphy, *Acquisitive crime and plastic card fraud: Findings from the 2008/09 British crime survey*, Home Office Statistical Bulletin (April 2010) at
http://rds.homeoffice.gov.uk/rds/pdfs10/hosb0810.pdf

Promontory Financial Group LLC and Wachtell, Lipton, Rosen & Katz, *Report to the Boards of Allied Irish Banks, p.l.c., Allfirst Financial Inc. and Allfirst Bank Concerning Currency Trading Losses* (12 March 2002), available at
http://info.worldbank.org/etools/docs/library/156006/pillars/pdfs/bib/ludwig.pdf

Alerts

Department of Homeland Security's United States Computer Emergency Readiness Team (US-CERT), Alert (TA14-002A) – *Malware Targeting Point of Sale Systems*, 2 January 2014, https://www.us-cert.gov/ncas/alerts/TA14-002A

Viruses

VRT Labs – Zeus Trojan Analysis,
http://labs.snort.org/papers/zeus.html

Kim Zetter, 'New ATM Malware Captures PINs and Cash — Updated', Wired, 6 April 2009
http://www.wired.com/threatlevel/2009/06/new-atm-malware-captures-pins-and-cash/

Selected press articles

2002
'Betting banker's "breathtaking" $19m sting', *Fairfax Digital*, 29 October 2002,
http://www.smh.com.au/articles/2003/10/29/1067233231668.html?from=storyrhs

2003
Philip Cornford and Sean Cowan, 'The mug punter who blew $18,998,309', *The Age*, 18 October 2003,
http://www.theage.com.au/articles/2003/10/17/1066364488821.html

'Bank manager's $19m sting sparks review', 31 October 2003, *Fairfax Digital*,
http://www.smh.com.au/articles/2003/10/31/1067566066203.html?from=storyrhs

2008
Matthew Taylor, 'Police think French pair tortured for pin details', *The Guardian*, 5 July 2008
http://www.guardian.co.uk/uk/2008/jul/05/knifecrime.ukcrime

2009
Andrew Beattie, 'Trading's 6 Biggest Losers', *Investopedia*, 26 February 26 2009,
http://www.investopedia.com/articles/trading/08/rogue-traders.asp

Elinor Mills with Tom Espiner, 'Hacked ATMs let criminals steal cash, PINs', *ZDNet*, 5 June 2009
http://www.zdnet.co.uk/news/security-threats/2009/06/05/hacked-atms-let-criminals-steal-cash-pins-39660339/

Kim Zetter, 'New ATM Malware Captures PINs and Cash — Updated', *Wired*, 4 June 2009
http://www.wired.com/threatlevel/2009/06/new-atm-malware-captures-pins-and-cash/

2009
'Bank worker fed £1m fraudsters with IDs', *Nottingham Post*, 22 May 2009
http://www.nottinghampost.com/Court-hears-1m-fraud-unraveled/story-12199246-detail/story.html

Bo Wilson, 'Grabbed by long arm of the law: fake cards crook threw from flat', *Evening Standard*, 23 October 2009
http://www.standard.co.uk/news/grabbed-by-long-arm-of-the-law-fake-cards-crook-threw-from-flat-6780156.html

2010
'Men jailed for Essex Pin number murder', BBC News, 13 May 2010,
http://news.bbc.co.uk/1/hi/england/essex/8679960.stm

Paul Cheston, 'Net "phishing" gang jailed for £1 million banking con', *Evening Standard*, 12 July 2011
http://www.standard.co.uk/news/net-phishing-gang-jailed-for-1-million-banking-con-6421021.html

'E-crime police arrest 19 over UK online bank theft', BBC News, 29 September 2012 http://www.bbc.co.uk/news/uk-11431989

Miles Brignall, 'Phantom cash machine withdrawals can haunt consumers' *The Guardian*, 16 October 2010
http://www.theguardian.com/money/2010/oct/16/cash-machine-withdrawals

2012
Rob Waugh, 'New banking cyber attack even penetrates accounts protected with latest PIN security devices' *Mail Online*, 6 February 2012
http://www.dailymail.co.uk/sciencetech/article-2097196/New-banking-cyber-attack-bypasses-passwords-latest-PIN-security-devices.html

Tara Evans, 'Barclays Bank admits blunder that led to account holder being blamed when £1,150 was stolen from her account', *Mail Online*, 22 June 2012,
http://www.dailymail.co.uk/news/article-2163287/Barclays-Bank-admits-blunder-led-account-holder-blamed-1-150-stolen-account.html

'Operation High Roller targets businesses and consumers with ability bypass multi-layer authentication', *SC Magazine*, 26 June 2012,
http://www.scmagazineuk.com/operation-high-roller-targets-

businesses-and-consumers-with-ability-bypass-multi-layer-authentication/article/247391/?DCMP=EMC-SCUK_Newswire

Cyrus Farivar, 'German security experts find major flaw in credit card terminals', *arstechnica*, 13 July 2012, http://arstechnica.com/security/2012/07/german-security-experts-find-major-flaw-in-credit-card-terminals/

Lee Boyce, "'I had £7.5k swiped from my account in six transactions but NatWest won't help me': Beware the online banking fraudsters", *This is Money*, 30 August 2012, up-dated 5 September 2012, http://www.thisismoney.co.uk/money/saving/article-2195342/I-7-5k-swiped-day-NatWest-wont-help-me.html

Tara Evans, 'Barclays blamed me for £10k fraud and then gave wrong evidence to the Financial Ombudsman' *This is Money*, 1 October 2012, http://www.thisismoney.co.uk/money/saving/article-2207787/Barclays-blamed-10k-fraud-gave-wrong-evidence-Financial-Ombudsman.html

Miles Brignall, 'Barclaycard theft leaves reader counting the cost of being pickpocketed', *The Guardian*, 5 October 2012, http://www.theguardian.com/money/2012/oct/05/pickpockets-pin-safe-barclays

Bob Howard, 'NatWest suspends Get Cash app' BBC News, 6 October 2012, http://www.bbc.co.uk/news/business-19857243

Courier Fraud Awareness Day http://content.met.police.uk/News/Courier-Fraud-Awareness-Day/1400015971764/1257246741786

2013

John Leyden, 'Bank Muscat hit by $39m ATM cash-out heist', The Register, 1 March 2013 http://www.theregister.co.uk/2013/03/01/bank_muscat_atm_mega_fraud/

'Vishing' scams net fraudsters £7m in one year, The Guardian, 28 August 2013 http://www.theguardian.com/money/2013/aug/28/vishing-scams-fraudsters-seven-million-pounds

'Vishing' and courier scam complaints increase, BBC News, 14 December 2013 http://www.bbc.co.uk/news/uk-25365698

2014

Paul Peachy, "'King of Acid' rave pioneer given five-year sentence for £1.25m bank cyber-fraud scheme', The Independent, 24 April 2014 http://www.independent.co.uk/news/uk/crime/king-of-acid-rave-pioneer-given-fiveyear-sentence-for-125m-bank-cyberfraud-scheme-9284346.html

'Vishing' scams net fraudsters £7m in one year, *The Guardian*, 28 August 2013
http://www.theguardian.com/money/2013/aug/28/vishing-scams-fraudsters-seven-million-pounds

John Leyden, 'Bank Muscat hit by $39m ATM cash-out heist', *The Register*, 1 March 2013
http://www.theregister.co.uk/2013/03/01/bank_muscat_atm_mega_fraud/

Index

Account security, 60
AID, 14
Allocation, court costs, 89
Allocation questionnaire, 88
   Return of, 91
Anti-virus software, 32
   Test of liability, as, 33
APACS see
   Financial Fraud Action UK
App, malware, 30
App Eff, 14
App Seq, 14
Appeal, right of, 96
Application Transaction Counter
   see ATC
ARPC, 11
ARQC, 11
ATC, 7
ATM System
   Action checklist, 98
   Card components, 5
   Customer guidance to avoid fraud, 127
   Employee theft, 17
   Encryption, undermining, 22
   Failure, 48
   False fronts, 23
   False keyboards, 26
   Legal position, detail, 134
   Network, 9
   Overview, 5
   Ownership, 9
   Particulars of claim for an ATM or PoS claim, 112
   Physical attacks, 16,17
   Pre-play attack, 20
   Process, 9
   Regularly targeted, 58
   Relay interception, 23
   Reversed transactions, 22
   Software recording errors, 21
   Thefts from, 15
   Transaction flow, 10-12
   Trapped cards, 23
Authcode, 13
Authorisation Request Cryptogram see ARQC
Authorisation Response Cryptogram see ARPC
Automated Teller Machine see ATM

Banking Conduct Regime, 40
Banking: Conduct of Business sourcebook, 58,71
Banks
   Burden of proof on, dispute, 68
   Contacting, after losses, 79
   Contract with, 39
      Unfair, 45
   Duties, 41,58
   Identification of customers, 61
   Investigation, 59,80
   Liability for error,
      Contractual, 39
      Refusal to accept, 2
   Litigation aims, 2
   Malware prevention, 31
   Negligence and, 47,58
   Questions to ask the bank, 119
   Response to legal action, 88
   Restoration of lost funds, 83
   Risks, ATM, controllable, 17
   Risks, ATM, partly controllable, 23,25
   Security systems, 60
   Transfers of funds. Identification and, 63
   Vulnerabilities, awareness of, 2
BCOBS see
Conduct of Business sourcebook
Burden of proof, dispute in, 68

CAP, 36
Card
   Authentication flow, 10
   Authentication key, 7
   Components, 5
   Customer duties, 42
   Data theft, 25
   Duplicate, 19
   Information stored, 6
   Lost, 39

Card *continued*
 Postal theft, 18,39
 Security standards, 75,76
 Stolen, 39
 Trapped, ATM, 23
Card Verification Value *see* CVV
Chip, 5,6
Chip Authentication Program
 see CAP
Civil Procedure Rules, 89
Claim, legal basis for, 67
Claim forms, 87
Cloned cards, 16
Common Criteria, card security, 75,76
Common indications, theft, 73
Computers, assumed to be in order, 77
Conduct of Business sourcebook, 58,71
Contacting bank, after losses, 79
Contactless cards, 8
 Refusing, 9
Contract with banks, 39
 Unfair, 45
Courier fraud, 27
Court,
 Allocation of track, 89
 Appeal, right of, 96
 Choice of, 87
 Costs, 87
 Disclosure, 92
 Expert, using, 94
 Hearing date, 91
 Letter before action, sample, 105
 Judgment, 96
 Preparing for, 94
 Witness statements, 95
Customer
 Duties, 42,48
  Protection against forgery, 49
 Identification of, 61
 Liability, card losses, 40
 Negligence and, 47
 PIN, 52-56
 Third party involvement, 48
CVV, 6,
 Magnetic strip and, 8

Debit, double, 39
Debit cards *see* ATM and PIN
Deposits, theft of, 22
Disabled people, courts and, 87
Disclosure, 2,92
 Questions to ask the bank, 119
Discovery *see* Disclosure
Dispute, handling, 79
Diverting the landline, theft and, 38
Double debit, 39
Drive by download, malware, 30

EFTSN, 13
Electronic banking
 see Internet banking
Electronic signature, PIN as, 5,68
Employee theft, 17
 Bank liability for losses, 39
EMV protocol, 19
Encryption, undermining PIN, 22
Evidence,
 Court, 95
  Detail, 163
 Destruction of, 2
 Digital, 41
 Disclosure, 2
 Expert, 94
 Preserving, 80
 Problems with, 73

Failure to inform bank, 44
False keyboards, 26
Financial Conduct Authority
 (FCA), 40
Financial Fraud Action UK figures, 44
Financial Ombudsman Service, 2,84
 PINs, 46
Financial Services and Markets
 Act 2000, 71
Forgery, duty of customer, 49
Fraud,
 Employee, 17,39
 Statistics, 130

Guessing a PIN, theft, 25

Home Office Counting Rules for fraud and forgery, 104
https prefix, 34
Human rights, European Convention, 94

Impersonating the bank, 37
Information Technology Security Evaluation Criteria (ITSEC), 75
Interception of information, 38
Internet banking
  Anti-virus software, 32
  CAP systems, 36
  Customer duties, 43
  Customer guidance to avoid fraud, 127
  Diverting the landline, 38
  Evidence, how courts approach it, detail, 163
  Impersonating the bank, 37
  Interception of information, 38
  Malware, 29
  Man in the middle attack, 32
  Particulars of claim for an internet banking claim, 108
  Personal information and, 38
  Phishing emails, 34
  Risks, 29
  Software updates, 32
  Texts, confirmatory, 36
  Theft, methods, 29
  Transaction Authentication Number, 37
  Weaknesses, 29
Internet shop safety, 33
Investigation of loss, bank, 59,80
Issue, device or card, 39
ITSEC *see* Information Technology Security Evaluation Criteria

Legal action, 85
  Allocation questionnaire, 88
  Bank's possible responses, 88
  Beginning, 87
  Claim forms, 87
  Costs, 87
  Disability, 87

Legal advice, 86
Letter before action, sample, 105
Mediation and negotiation, 85
Particulars of claim for an ATM or PoS claim, 112
Particulars of claim for an internet banking claim, 108
Time limit, 85
Legal advice, 86
  Questions to ask before instruction, 116
Letter before action, sample, 105
Liability
  Bank, 39
  Consumer, 40
Limitation on action, 85
Links and further information, 181
Loss, nature of, 67
Lost cards, 39

Magnetic strip, 5,7
  Fallback for ATMs, 13
Malware, 29
  Capability, 31
  How it is placed, 30
  Prevention, banks, 31
  Prevention, consumer, 32
Man in the middle attack, 32
Mediation and negotiation, 85
MID, 13

Negligence, 47
  Bank, 58
  Failure of ATM, 48
  Failure of back end systems, 48
  Thief obtains data, 48
  Third party involvement, 48
No PIN attack, 19

Observing PIN entry, theft, 26
Online banking *see* Internet banking
Overriding Objective, 93

Padlock signs, websites, 33
PAN, 6
Patterns of spending, unusual, 61
Pay per install malware, 30

Payment Services
  Regulations, 40,69,83
Personal Identification Number
  see PIN
Personal information, obtaining
  for theft, 38
Phishing emails, 34
PIN, 5
  Action checklist, 98
  APACS advice, 76
  Customer duties, 42,52
  Disguising, 56,57
  Electronic signature, as, 5,68
  Financial Ombudsman
    Service advice, 46
  Function, 50
  Guessing, theft, 25
  Impersonating the bank, theft by, 37
  Legal position, detail, 134
  Magnetic strip, 8
  Observing entry, theft, 26
  Postal theft, 18
  Revealing, forcible, 17
  Smartphones, 27
  Software recording errors, 21
  Tampered entry devices, 27
  Verification flaws, 19
Point of Sale (PoS) claims see PIN
Police involvement, 83,84
Pre-play attack, 20
Principal Account Number see PAN
Prudential Regulation Authority
  (PRA), 40
PTID, 13

Ram raid, 17
Receipts, ATM, 13
Relay interception, 23
Reporting theft, 83
Restoration of lost funds, 83
Reversed transactions, 22
Risks,
  ATM, controllable by banks, 17
  ATM, partly controllable by
    banks, 23,25
  ATM, controllable by users, 27

Secure Socket Layer see SSL
Shoulder surfing, 26
Skimming data, 15
Smartphones, 27
SSL, 33
Static Data Authentication, 10
Stolen cards, 39

TAN see Transaction
  Authentication Number
TC, 12
Theft, reporting, 83
Theft of deposits, 22
TID, 13
Transaction Authentication
  Number, 37
Transaction Certificate see TC
Transfers of funds. Identification
  and, 63

UDK, 7
Unfair Contract Terms
Unique Derived Key see UDK

Verification of cards,
  ATM, by, 11
  Flaws in, 19
Virtual keyboards, 37
Vishing fraud, 28

Witness statements, 95

Zero-day threats, 32
Zero-hour threats, 32

Lightning Source UK Ltd.
Milton Keynes UK
UKOW04f0126101014

239851UK00001B/66/P

9 781858 117218